Other books by Steve Case:

Hands-on Service Ideas for Youth

It's My Choice, Teacher's

It's My Choice, Student

Time Out

To order, call 1-800-765-6955.

Visit us at

www.reviewandherald.com

for information on other Review and Herald products.

Steve Case

REVIEW AND HERALD® PUBLISHING ASSOCIATION
HAGERSTOWN, MD 21740

Edited by Lori Peckham
Designed by Trent Truman
Cover illustration by Sean Parkes
Electronic makeup by Shirley M. Bolivar
Typeset: 11/13 Cheltenham

PRINTED IN U.S.A.

06 05 04 03 02   5 4 3 2 1

R&H Cataloging Service
Case, Steve, 1957-
    On the case.

    1. Christian life.   2. Religious life.   I. Title.

            248.486732

ISBN 0-8280-1603-8

Marvin and Billie Ann Case
("Dad" and "Mom" to me).
Because of you I've always felt it was OK
to ask questions.
And you also modeled for me
an eagerness to search for answers.

INTRODUCTION

GOD AND ME

OUR SPECIAL DAY

STICKY SPIRITUAL ISSUES

WHAT'S WRONG WITH . . . ?

PEOPLE PROBLEMS

LIVING FOR HIM

CONCLUSION
SCRIPTURE INDEX

INTRO-
DUCTION

"I've got a question" is music to my ears. And that's not because I feel as if I have all the answers. I like the statement because *I love discovery.* When someone has a question, it means that person is open to discovering something they don't know or understand. When someone asks me a question, I usually discover something in the process, too.

Young people seem to be ready to take in so much! For those who have grown up going to church, it's a time when you no longer just take what other people have been saying for years. You look for freshness and relevance, openness and application. Game-playing and repeating the party line won't cut it with the youth. I love that! It's great to be real; it's great to be honest!

Let me be clear about not knowing all the answers to questions young people have. One text I rely on is Deuteronomy 29:29 (TLB), "There are secrets the Lord your God has not revealed to us, but these words which he has revealed are for us and our children to obey forever."

In other words, there are some things God still hasn't shown us. But there are lots of things He's already made plain. I'm so thankful that we have the Bible so we can better understand and live for God.

I have a special thank you for *Insight* magazine for asking me to write the On the Case column for their weekly publication. They have been so patient with me on deadlines, and then they take my feeble attempts to answer real questions and edit them. *Thank you,* Lori

Peckham and Michelle Sturm!

When I answered the questions in this book, I was writing based on e-mail or letters that came by snail mail. Since there wasn't a living person for me to interact with, I would imagine some of the young people who have been in my youth groups or those who go on mission trips with me or those I cross paths with at Bible conferences or other youth gatherings. I know the questions are real, and so I imagine the young people I know and then write as though they were sitting across the desk from me and we're having a conversation.

Based on the responses I've received from those who read *Insight,* the answers I give frequently apply to your situation. Sometimes they miss the mark, and sometimes they miss by a long shot. For that I apologize. I'm hopeful that you'll ask again, or find another person to respond for you. Fortunately, God isn't dependent on me to be the only source for giving you answers. I'm just grateful for the privilege to be one resource that's available.

The most frequent question I'm asked is some form of "What's wrong with . . . ?" You can put whatever you want in that blank. It's usually a lifestyle issue such as dancing, jewelry, and going to the theater. I figure that a parent or other authority person has told you that you can't do it (whatever "it" is) and you want to do it, so you're looking for someone to give you some reasons to get what you want. Some people just want to be in a tug of war with others, but some people want some straight answers to direct their lives.

I purposely answer some of these questions with a somewhat nebulous response. That can frustrate someone looking for a quick "yes" or "no" answer so they can agree or disagree. I usually don't find the issues to be as easy as "yes" or "no." Often the questions don't have a neat Bible text that matches, unless you use only one verse and ignore many others. A well-thought-out answer might depend on a number of things. Besides, you've already had the answers given to you as a child. The reason you have the questions again is that the childish answers aren't adequate for you any longer (see 1 Corinthians 13:11, 12).

The purpose of this book is for young people to have a place to ask questions that are important to them, and then to find answers from a Biblical and pastoral perspective. We want the answers to come from the authority of God (the Bible) and with the understanding of a Person who genuinely cares (Psalm 23 and Hebrews 4:15, 16).

Insight magazine will continue its column On the Case, but that covers only one question each week. By owning this resource, you have at your fingertips a bunch of questions and answers that you can refer to, especially when they are the very questions you're asking at that moment.

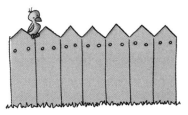

GOD AND ME

IS GOD REALLY THERE?

*How do you know that God is there
when you can't see or hear His presence?*

During my childhood I constantly felt my parents' presence—whether through their kisses, hugs, spankings, or words. When it came to adolescence, though, I didn't see or hear my parents as much as before. But that doesn't mean they weren't still acting on my behalf. And much of who I am and what I am today comes from their years of giving me input.

My parents showed me the way early in life, just as yours probably did for you. But as you become independent of the very ones who gave you life, you need to transfer your dependence to the One who *really* gives you life.

God isn't as visible or audible as your parents. But you can learn to hear His voice and see His actions. It's kind of like starting over as a kid. What history do you have with God? Where have you seen and heard Him in the past?

Some people find direction from a passage such as Isaiah 30:20, 21: The Lord "is your teacher, and he will not continue to hide from you. You will see your teacher with your own eyes. If you go the wrong way—to the right or to the left—you will hear a voice behind you. It will say, 'This is the right way. You should go this way'" (EB).

I haven't heard that voice. Others I know have heard it. Some have developed a prayer life that makes them sensitive to get messages from God.

For me, I take greater comfort in Hebrews 1:1, 2: "Long ago God spoke in many different ways to our fathers through the prophets [in visions, dreams, and even face to face], telling them little by little about his plans. But now in these days He has spoken to us through his Son" (TLB).

When I read the Bible, especially the Gospels (Matthew, Mark, Luke, and John), I get a good idea of what God is like—so I can "hear" and "see" Him.

I'm really looking forward to seeing God face-to-face when He returns. Until then, my faith is based on what He has done for others as well as for me.

How Can I Know God Personally?

*We're told it's possible to have a
personal relationship with God. But how?*

When you develop relationships with other people, you find ways to get to know them. You hang out with them, do things they like to do, watch them, talk to them, and listen to them.

And as you get to know other people, you might decide they aren't all you thought they were. Or you might find out they're even better than you'd hoped.

It's when you get to know a person that your relationship becomes personal. Before that, it's based on what someone else thinks or says.

14

The same is true of your relationship with God. If you grow up as a Christian, your relationship with God is based on what others tell you—people like your parents, teachers, pastors, or other adults.

So how do you get to know God for yourself—personally? Here are some ways that have worked for me:

• READ YOUR BIBLE. Instead of reading your Bible as a textbook, read it as a letter from God to you. Or read it as a story about the Person (God) you're trying to get to know.

Try reading Mark or 1 John. You may even want to mark your Bible or jot notes in the margin regarding your new discoveries about God. You'll have to create time for this, since I don't know many teens who have loads of extra time to fill.

• PRAY. Talk to God about what you've read in the Bible, or about what's happening in your life. Some people find that writing their prayers in a journal makes their communication with God more personal.

• TEAM UP WITH ANOTHER PERSON WHO ALSO WANTS TO GET TO KNOW GOD PERSONALLY. Check in with each other about how it's going and what you're discovering. Bottling up your new knowledge kills it; talking about it feeds it.

• OPEN YOUR EYES AND SEE GOD'S INVOLVEMENT IN YOUR WORLD. Sometimes we don't look for or recognize God acting in situations. So try looking for His activity and learn from what it tells you about Him.

• RELATIONSHIPS TAKE TIME. A personal relationship is an investment, not a crash course. Give it time—at least a month or two; six months is even better. Then please let me know about the God you've discovered through your personal relationship with Him.

Here's God's message to all of us: "'You will seek me and find me when you seek me with all your heart. I will be found by you,' declares the Lord" (Jeremiah 29:13, 14).

If God isn't your personal God, start seeking Him with all your heart. He wants you to know Him personally too!

WHEN THINGS GO WRONG

*How can you stay close to God
when everything seems to be going wrong?*

When everything seems to be going wrong, where else are you going to go other than to God?

I've heard plenty of testimonies about how God has saved people from bad situations. It goes something like "My life was a mess; everything was going wrong. Then I met Jesus, and everything has been great."

My reaction to those testimonies is "Hallelujah!" and "Enjoy it, because it won't last!"

Please don't get me wrong. I'm completely in favor of getting with Jesus and staying with Him. I just don't find that most Christians have a trouble-free life. And the Bible clues us in on that as well. Here are a few words from four of the Bible writers.

• "Everyone who wants to live a godly life in Christ Jesus will be persecuted" (2 Timothy 3:12).

• "Blessed are you when people insult you, persecute you and falsely say all kinds of evil against you because of me" (Matthew 5:11).

• "To this you were called, because Christ suffered for you, leaving you an example, that you should follow in his steps" (1 Peter 2:21).

• "In this world you will have trouble. But take heart! I have overcome the world" (John 16:33).

I wish I could promise you trouble-free bliss. But that's heaven, not sinful earth. So until we get to heaven, keep in mind these three basic truths for staying close to God when everything seems to be going wrong:

1. ALL PEOPLE HAVE BAD THINGS HAPPEN TO THEM (Christians and non-Christians alike). Being a Christian doesn't remove you from this world; it just gives you a different perspective. Being a non-Christian doesn't make life easy either—it's a jungle out there!

2. THE BENEFIT OF BEING CLOSE TO GOD WHEN THINGS GO WRONG IS THAT YOU'RE NOT ALONE—HE'S THERE WITH YOU. And so are many other Christians. In fact, getting together with other Christians to build each other up is a better reason for going to church than showing off your latest threads or catching up on gossip.

3. IT'S UP TO YOU TO CHOOSE EITHER TO STAY WITH GOD DURING THE BAD TIMES OR TO TRY IT ON YOUR OWN. I've found that making time for personal devotions (my own time with God) is what tilts the scale for me. I'm praying that that will be your experience too!

DOES GOD SPEAK TO ME?

How can you tell if God's telling you something, or if it's just a thought of your own?

One of the participants on a mission trip probably didn't realize how often she said it, but every other phrase began with "God told me."

I doubted that God really said all the things she shared. So I pressed her to identify how she could tell if her messages truly were from God.

She hedged for quite a while. Finally she explained, "When I have a thought, I wonder if it's from God. So I always pray a little prayer that goes like this: 'Dear God, if this thought is from You, help me to think it again.' Then if I think that thought again, it must be from God."

Sound incredible? I thought so. It seems more like the power of suggestion than a message from heaven. Her constant referencing to "God told me" reminded me of blasphemy more than spirituality.

I admire people who have developed the art of listening to hear God's voice. They often meditate and spend time in solitude to discern God's voice.

I haven't done so well at that myself. I'm most apt to get a message from God by reading the Bible. Second Timothy 3:16, 17 puts it this way: "The whole Bible was given to us by inspiration from God and is useful to teach us what is true and to make us realize what is wrong in our lives; it straightens us out and helps us do what is right. It is God's way of making us well prepared at every point, fully equipped to do good to everyone" (TLB).

I like checking thoughts I have with what God has already told us (the Bible). That prevents me from doing my own thing and then claiming, "God told me."

You may also want to check out a book titled *Testimonies for the Church* written by Ellen White. In volume 5 Mrs. White helps us know how God guides us. She writes, "There are three ways in which the Lord reveals His will to us. . . . God reveals His will to us in His word, the Holy Scriptures. His voice is also revealed in His providential workings. . . . Another way in which God's voice is heard is through the appeals of His Holy Spirit, making impressions upon the heart. . . . If you are in doubt upon any subject you must first consult the Scriptures" (p. 512).

AM I HOLDING BACK?

How do you deal with something in your life
that you might be kind of unwilling to do for God
if it was necessary, but you don't really feel
it is necessary? Is that like holding back something
from God instead of giving Him your all?

Let me get this straight. You're thinking of something you don't want to do. And you're hoping God doesn't mind, since it really isn't necessary right now. Does that mean you're holding back?

I'm dying to know what this thing is. But let me plug in two very different examples and see what happens.

Let's say you've read the story of Jesus calling the disciples to leave their nets and follow him (Mark 1:16-18). You're impressed by how quickly they responded. Then you come across the story of the rich young ruler (Mark 10:17-22). Jesus asked him to sell all he had, give it to the poor, and then follow Him.

You feel convicted as you read, and the question forms in your mind: "Should I sell all I have and follow Jesus?" That means selling your Walkman, your bike, most of your clothes, and maybe your CDs. After giving the money to the poor, you'll follow Jesus.

Where will you go? What will you do?

Maybe it's not time to become homeless. Perhaps you shouldn't drop out of high school right now and become a street preacher. Maybe it isn't really necessary to do all of this.

Does this mean you're holding back? Do you just have to be "willing" to be like the rich young ruler, but not actually do it?

19

Let's try another example. You're reminded of the demon-possessed man whom Jesus set free (Mark 5:1-20). After being healed, the man asked Jesus if he could follow Him. But Jesus told the man to go home to his family and tell them how much the Lord had done for him (see Mark 5:19).

If you take this story to heart, you wouldn't sell your stuff and hit the road for Jesus. Instead, you'd stay home and share Jesus with your family.

So which should you do?

For those who want a neat and specific formula, you won't get it here. God made you a unique person, so you can expect that His desires for you are created especially for you.

If you must have a formula, here's what you can anticipate: following Jesus will take all you have, and you'll need the supernatural power of God for it to become a reality.

You might go through years of preparation before the supernatural becomes obvious. Like Daniel, it might not be until things go really bad (being taken captive) that you'll see that all those years of investment with God prepared you for the next step.

In the meantime, here are a few ideas that have worked well for me.

• Make a commitment of yourself completely to God.

• Do your absolute best in whatever you're doing right now.

• Keep on the lookout for what God is doing in your life and around you.

HOW CAN JESUS FEEL REAL?

*I know Jesus is real, but how can I feel like
He's a friend to me right now, not just
some person in the Bible?*

Here are two ways you can feel Jesus' friendship:
   1. MAKE JESUS PART OF YOUR EVERYDAY LIFE. Start
the day by inviting Him into your life. Then carry on a
conversation with Him all day. Talk (even silently) to
Him about what you're doing and why you're doing it.
Ask Jesus to lead you in a way that you'll sense His reality, then start watching for it.

Ask others what makes Jesus seem real to them. We
talk about religion and the facts of Jesus' existence, but
we don't often talk about what's going on personally
between Jesus and us.

Look for Jesus in the form of people who are in need
(see Matthew 25:35-40). Look and listen for Him in others who reach out to you. Look and listen for Him in nature, in Scripture, and in prayer.

Make a pact with a friend to share where you've
seen Jesus after one week. Maybe you'll want to do this
every week. Setting a date to share with a friend makes
us accountable and nudges us to follow through on
what we want to do.

Each night review what happened during your day
with Jesus, and let that be your "bedtime prayer."
   2. IMAGINE YOURSELF AS A CHARACTER IN THE BIBLE STO-
RIES YOU READ. Those old stories may seem unreal to
you, especially since you don't live in a culture like the
one described in the Bible.

Get a fresh Bible and treat it as a personal letter

from God to you. I'd recommend a paraphrase such as *The Message* or *The Clear Word,* especially if you already have most Bible stories memorized.

Don't just race through the pages to see how quickly you can finish reading them. Take one story at a time, and use your sanctified imagination to play one of the characters' parts. Then read the story again and put yourself in a different role.

Start with a book like Mark. Then try John, Matthew, and Luke. I like many of the Old Testament stories, too, like the ones in 2 Kings 2. The story of Elijah going to heaven in a fiery chariot takes some great imagination. I really like the part in which Elisha smacks the Jordan River with Elijah's coat and asks, "Where now is the Lord, the God of Elijah?" (2 Kings 2:14).

Mark your new Bible with notes, underlinings, highlights, and other comments. You may even want to start a study journal. Describe what your imagination came up with. Include your thoughts, feelings, questions, hopes, and even frustrations. Your journaling can be your prayer for that day.

Try these suggestions, but feel free to add your own. And get ready to feel Jesus' friendship grow inside you!

FORGIVE AND FORGET?

Does Jesus really forget our sins when He forgives us? What if someone has sex, asks for forgiveness, then keeps having sex with different people? Does God keep forgiving and forgetting?

Holy amnesia! What's going on here? First, let's consider some texts that talk about God "forgetting" our sins.

Jeremiah 31:34 quotes the Lord, saying, "I will forgive their wickedness and will remember their sins no more." And Micah 7:19 says about God, "You will tread our sins underfoot and hurl all our iniquities into the depths of the sea."

When people confess their sins to God, He's promised to forgive them (1 John 1:9). But sometimes people don't seem to forgive themselves (maybe because they don't feel forgiven).

When I counsel people with that problem, I emphasize the concept of holy amnesia. I point out that when we ask God to forgive us for the umpteenth time for something we did 10 years ago, God doesn't know what we're talking about! Why? Because He's forgiven (erased) the sin.

But does that mean that God's "computer hard drive" has also been erased?

Well, suppose a guy has sex with his girlfriend, then feels guilty about it. He confesses his sin to God, and God forgives him. So does God remember the sin?

Now, what if two weeks later the girl also knows she sinned and confesses her sin to God? Will God say "I have no idea what you're talking about"?

We can push it even further. Suppose the girl becomes pregnant as a result of their sexual promiscuity and gives birth. Will God not know where the baby came from because He "forgave and forgot" the parents' sin? Sounds pretty ridiculous, doesn't it?

Actually, Malachi 3:16 mentions a "book of remembrance," where positive things are recorded. And in the story of the sheep and goats (Matthew 25:31-46), Jesus recalls whether or not each person has served others.

But because Satan accuses us day and night before God (Revelation 12:10), it's comforting to know that God keeps records! That way He can point out to Satan that our sins have been forgiven because we confessed them to Him.

Our sins are gone in terms of God resurrecting them. But God has accurate records so the devil won't pull a number on us!

For those who fall into a cycle of sinning—asking forgiveness, then committing the same sin again—I recommend taking to heart 1 John 3:4-10 in *The Message*. Part of it reads, "People conceived and brought into life by God don't make a practice of sin. How could they? God's seed is deep within them, making them who they are."

MY RELATIONSHIP WITH GOD IS UP AND DOWN

*I love God with all my heart. So I just don't
understand why I'm not living the lifestyle
that a Christian should live. It seems as though
I live my Christian life for maybe a day or two,
and then I go right back to saying and doing
things I know I shouldn't. What can I do to
change my life and begin to live with God 24/7?*

You can live with God 24/7, but that doesn't mean your life will be one steady plateau from now on.

Consider Elijah. In 1 Kings 18 Elijah leads all of Israel from worshiping Baal back to worshiping Yahweh, the true God. I love to imagine what it must have been like on Mount Carmel, when the fire came down at Elijah's request and consumed the sacrifice, the wood, the rocks, the water, and even the dirt! And then the rain came! Awesome!

It sounds as if everything was looking great for both Elijah and God. Talk about an emotional high after a very spiritual experience!

But that very night Elijah experienced an emotional

crash when he heard that Jezebel was out to kill him. He ran the equivalent of three marathons to get away. And then he became suicidal! In 1 Kings 19:4 we read that Elijah prayed, "'I have had enough, Lord,' . . . 'Take my life; I am no better than my ancestors.'"

It's happened to me many times, and I've seen it happen to others, too. It occurs after a mission trip or a prayer conference or other retreat has sort of worn off. The desire for God seems to dwindle, and people start messing up again.

Elijah went to Mount Horeb (also called Mount Sinai) to find God again. So it's probably a good idea to return to a place where you know God has been revealed to you before.

But on Mount Horeb God now came to Elijah via a "still small voice." So it might be that God is communicating with you when you're not even aware of it, because He's doing it in a way you didn't expect!

God wants to have a relationship with us. But we have to make choices daily that take us either toward God or away from Him.

Isn't it amazing that we sometimes demand to make our own choices, but when God keeps giving us the freedom to choose we grow tired and let others make bad or simply lazy choices for us?

I'm not a surfer, but I've talked to a number of them, and they've shared with me things about surfing that I think relate to living the Christian life 24/7. I call it "surfer theology." See if you can make the application to living for God.

• If you're a surfer, you're always a surfer, even if you aren't surfing at that moment.

• As a surfer you ride the wave and enjoy it for as long as you can, even though you know it will eventually come to an end.

• When you crash you don't quit—you go right back

out to catch another wave.

• No two waves are exactly the same. Each wave is a unique experience.

• You spend most of your time waiting for the next big one.

• When the right wave comes, you have to paddle like crazy to catch it.

• It's definitely worth it.

AM I READY FOR BAPTISM?

When should I be ready for baptism? I've taken three baptismal classes, but am still not allowed.

Get baptized when you're ready to get married to Jesus.

That may sound questionable, especially if you're a guy! But I'm actually (sort of) serious about this.

You know the big three questions for young people, don't you? (Not "What shall I wear?" "Who will be there?" "Is there any food?")

1. WILL I CHOOSE TO FOLLOW JESUS FOR MYSELF (not just my parents' choice for me)?

2. WHAT WILL MY FIRST VOCATION BE? (What will I be when I grow up?)

3. WHOM WILL I MARRY (if I do)?

Your question about baptism relates to the first big question.

For many adults baptism is the symbol of becoming a Christian. At one time John the Baptist used this to symbolize that people wanted a new start in their spiritual life (see Mark 1:4). Just as going under the water "washed away the dirt," symbolically a person's sins were "washed away."

Later Peter baptized people not only to forgive their past sins but also for them to "receive the gift of the Holy Spirit" (Acts 2:38).

Those who grow up in the Adventist Church probably have asked to have their sins forgiven hundreds of times before baptism—maybe every day! So if you've grown up in the church, baptism symbolizes the start of a new phase in your life. It means you have made the decision on your own.

This is where the marriage thing comes in. When a person gets married, it should be because they are choosing their partner for life, not because parents are pressuring them or because they're just sort of slipping into a lifelong rut with a person.

The same is true for your baptism. When you say yes to Jesus for yourself, the baptism is your wedding ceremony, and the Holy Spirit (God) comes into your life as your partner. Are you ready for that?

Going through a baptismal class can be like premarriage counseling. Make sure you get more than just information about God. Find out how to grow in your relationship with Jesus after the wedding/baptism.

I wonder if the reason you're "not allowed" to be baptized is because some of the people close to you don't think you're ready for a marriage to Jesus. Ask them why and explain where you're coming from, especially why you honestly want to be baptized.

This is a big time to be sure. It's much more than a Sabbath swim! It's your wedding with Jesus.

WHAT NEXT?

*I've heard lots of stuff about giving your life to
God and getting right with God, but it seems
as if I never hear anything about what to do
after that. How can I get closer to God
after I've given my life to Him?*

Some people try to get closer to God without ever giving their life to Him in the first place. That's definitely backward, as you know!

But then some people give their lives to God and stop right there. They figure that since they accepted Him back in 1998, they can coast from now on.

But you sense that there's more to it than that. And you're right! So, what is it?

Paul told some early believers, "And now just as you trusted Christ to save you, trust him, too, for each day's problems; live in vital union with him. Let your roots grow down into him and draw up nourishment from him. See that you go on growing in the Lord, and become strong and vigorous in the truth you were taught. Let your lives overflow with joy and thanksgiving for all he has done" (Colossians 2:6, 7, TLB).

Actually, don't stop there. I recommend reading the whole book of Colossians. (It's short.)

Now, let's look at your relationship with God somewhat like a relationship with a close friend. Once you become friends with someone, then what do you do? You probably spend time doing things that both of you enjoy. And sometimes you just like being together. As you spend time together, you find out more about each other; you even "rub off" on each other.

But there's not just one way to do friendship. It's something you explore and experience together.

The same is true with the relationship you've started with Jesus. As far as doing things together is concerned, you can expect that you'll be doing some of the things Jesus did, because that's what He still enjoys doing. He'll even give you special abilities to do these things! (See 1 Corinthians 12.)

Two other texts provide insight into this subject. In Ephesians 2:8-10 you'll discover that when you gave your life to God, He gave you eternal life and heaven as a gift. Beyond that, He's turned your life into poetry ("workmanship" in the KJV; "poie⁻ma" in Greek, from which we get the word "poem").

Also, 2 Corinthians 5:17-21 says that when you became friends with God, you automatically became His ambassador to bring other friends to Him. So whom do you know who isn't friends with God? Introduce them!

Then there are the fruits of the Spirit. Check out Galatians 5:22, 23. In those verses Paul talks about the fact that when you became friends with God, the Holy Spirit began living inside of you. And He'll develop spiritual fruit in you over time.

They're good fruits, too: love, joy, peace, patience, kindness, goodness, faithfulness, gentleness, and self-control. How open are you to having the Holy Spirit develop these qualities in you?

Stick with your relationship with Jesus. Be open to do the things He did, and become like Him in your character. He's already saved you. Now He'll continue to transform you. What a friend!

AM I SAVED?

How can I know I'll go to heaven and not hell?

Some say we'll never know for sure until Jesus returns. Others say we can know now. Still others say it's none of our business. But just about everyone wants to know at one time or another whether or not they'll be going to heaven or hell.

Underline this passage in your Bible: 1 John 5:11-13. Write the text in the back or front of your Bible for easy reference. This is the text I turn to when I'm uncertain about where I'm going when everything is said and done.

Here's what verses 11 and 12 say in *The Living Bible.* "And what is it that God has said? That he has given us eternal life, and that this life is in his Son. So whoever has God's Son has life; whoever does not have his Son, does not have life."

That's it. If you have God's Son, you have (eternal) life. If you don't have His Son, you don't. Put in the form of an equation, it looks like this:

You + God's Son = eternal life

You − God's Son = no eternal life

But sometimes I wonder if I *really* have God's Son. When in doubt, I simply pray for Jesus to come into my life again, just in case I've somehow edged Him out. That's a prayer God always answers with an immediate "yes." So I do have God's Son, which means I have eternal life.

I think John put in verse 13 for those of us who think this is too good to be true. It reads, "I have written this to you who believe in the Son of God so that you may know you have eternal life" (TLB). For those who want another text, the same writer, John, wrote that those who believe in Jesus have already passed from death to life (see John 5:24). Another similar message is in Romans 8:1.

If you wonder whether or not you have Jesus, just pray and ask Him to come into your heart right *now!*

No need to be hopelessly uncertain. In John 14:2, 3 Jesus assured us, "In my Father's house are many rooms; if it were not so, I would have told you. I am going to prepare a place for you. And if I go and prepare a place for you, I will come back and take you to be with me that you also may be where I am."

In Ephesians 1:13, 14, the Scripture says that the Holy Spirit in your life is the down payment that God will take you to heaven when Jesus returns.

God already made provision for your salvation and is preparing a place for you. He's chosen you as His child. The only question you need to deal with is Are you His?

OUR SPECIAL DAY

WHAT'S OK ON SABBATH?

What are things that are OK to do on Sabbath?

The religious leaders asked Jesus the same question. He told them it was OK ("lawful" or "permitted" or "right") to do good on the Sabbath (Matthew 12:12).

What a concept. It's OK to do good things on Sabbath!

But you want to know: What are "good" things?

First, some people get so uptight about possibly breaking the Sabbath that they basically do nothing. Some are so worried about doing the right thing that they spend most of the Sabbath trying to figure out if what they want to do is on the approved list of Sabbath activities.

If you've grown up as a Seventh-day Adventist, whatever rules you had as a child often become the standard for you. For example, I just know that it's not OK to go white-water rafting on Sabbath. Why? It's just not, that's why!

If you press me, I'd come up with some lame reason such as "It's too active" or "It's too much fun for Sabbath." But the main reason is that I just didn't do it growing up, so it must be wrong.

Our Sabbath rules come from the Seventh-Day

Baptists, who got their ideas from the Puritans in England. They knew that Sabbath was a day for not working. But since children didn't work, what would the Sabbath command be for *them?*

A child's full-time job is play, so Sabbath must be a day for no playing. That's why some Adventist youth won't shoot a basket on Sabbath without calling out a Bible name. But many European (not British) Adventists play recreational games on Sabbath—they don't think it's wrong to play on Sabbath.

One of our biggest "stumbling blocks" for what's OK on Sabbath is a misuse of not "doing your own pleasure" (Isaiah 58:13, NASB). It seems to get passed on that "if you like it, it must be wrong." But if I like to go to church, then it must be the wrong thing to do on Sabbath. If I don't like to go to church, then it must be a great Sabbath activity. How ridiculous!

The very next phrase in the same verse is "call the Sabbath a delight." If Sabbath's not a pleasure, how can it be called a delight?

Our hang-up seems to be the word pleasure. Some translations use the word business, so it reads, in effect, "Not doing your own business, but calling the Sabbath delight."

In other words, don't settle merely for doing acceptable things on Sabbath; instead, do the very best things on Sabbath.

What are the best things to do on Sabbath? The context of Isaiah 58 gives the answer: set people free by serving others on Sabbath. Remember, it's OK to do good on the Sabbath!

CAN I WORK ON SABBATH?

Is it OK to do volunteer work on Sabbath,
like fire fighting or other community service?

I can see why you asked that question. The issue is confusing because it seems to create a conflict between two "Sabbath principles."

• **PRINCIPLE ONE:** Sabbath is *not* a day for work. According to the fourth commandment, we have six days to do our work, "but the seventh day is a Sabbath to the Lord your God. On it you shall not do any work" (Exodus 20:10). That chapter goes on to say that everyone in your household—family, servants, immigrants, and even animals—shouldn't work on Sabbath!

• **PRINCIPLE TWO:** Sabbath *is* a day for helping others. One Sabbath Jesus healed a woman who'd been crippled for 18 years. But the synagogue ruler told everyone, "There are six days for work. So come and be healed on those days, not on the Sabbath" (Luke 13:14).

Jesus pointed out, however, that if animals receive basic care on Sabbath, shouldn't people (children of God) receive even better care, especially on Sabbath? The people rejoiced over Jesus' response and the woman's healing, but the leaders felt humiliated.

Seventh-day Adventists take seriously the Sabbath command not to do any work on the seventh day. But because Jesus healed a number of people on Sabbath, we've determined that medical work is OK during Sabbath hours. Rarely have we extended the principle of helping others beyond medical services.

While we should help others every day, Sabbath is especially suited for that. But a note of caution: don't let a service attitude overshadow the worship you give your Creator on Sabbath. Certainly there is adequate time for both, especially when you plan ahead how you're going to spend your Sabbath.

If you push the boundaries of helping others beyond medical or emergency "work" on Sabbath, you can expect at least minor "persecution," although it won't be nearly as intense as what Jesus experienced (see John 5:16).

But remember, most Adventist churches have loads of volunteer "workers" who provide leadership and services on Sabbath so the programs can take place (Sabbath school teachers, deacons, potluck coordinators). So why not include some form of service to benefit those outside your church on Sabbath?

Isaiah said that we would find our joy in the Lord not only by doing religious activities but by helping others (Isaiah 58:13, 14). He especially points out the blessing of serving others on Sabbath instead of simply doing our own thing (verse 13).

What a challenge for us today—to go beyond religious actions, doing only what we want to do, and actually experiencing joy in the Lord by serving those He created and died for.

What are you doing to serve others after church this Sabbath? Remember, the Sabbath is about four things:

• REST (a change from what you do the other days of the week)
• WORSHIP (of the Creator)
• JOY (celebrating being with God)
• SERVICE (restoring God's creation)

WEDDINGS AND FUNERALS ON SABBATH

Is it wrong to attend a wedding or a funeral on Sabbath?
Is it wrong to have a wedding or a funeral on Sabbath?

The first wedding on this planet could have taken place on the first Sabbath (Friday night of Creation week). You'd think a wedding would be a positive spiritual experience, especially because Sabbath and marriage are two gifts God gave us in the Garden of Eden.

I've attended some weddings that were highly spiritual, and I've been to others that weren't. Sometimes you know what to expect in advance based on the people involved.

And frequently the wedding reception has a very different atmosphere from the wedding. Perhaps you might want to attend a Sabbath wedding, but not the reception.

Funerals can blend nicely with Sabbath, especially if the service inspires hope during a time of loss and grief. And many services remind us that our Creator will make all things new at the end of the world.

But anyone who has put on a wedding or a funeral will quickly admit that there's a world of difference between *attending* these services and *preparing* for them. Many people wouldn't want the stress on Sabbath that comes from putting on either event.

At my own wedding I didn't feel a lot of stress for two reasons. First, because brides typically take on more responsibility for weddings, and I was the groom. Second, because my best man worked like crazy on my wedding day so I didn't have to. (I had done the same for him one month earlier.)

Weddings or funerals also necessitate a fair amount

of work on the part of church members, who help set things up, oversee various tasks during the event, and clean up afterward. Also, on a practical level, scheduling conflicts are more likely if you try to squeeze in a wedding or a funeral on Sabbath.

For the weddings I've attended at 3:00 on a Sunday afternoon, the hosts started preparing on Saturday night and worked all Sunday morning. Funerals take less time to prepare, because the family usually hires the services of a funeral home.

So I may consider it appropriate or even desirable to attend a wedding or a funeral on Sabbath. But who will do all the work of preparing for it? Often the issue of preparation outweighs the benefits of doing these activities on Sabbath.

Special planning to take care of all the preparations before sundown might make it worthwhile to experience these significant events on Sabbath. Or perhaps we need simpler weddings. Anyone in favor of having the wedding right during the church service?

KEEPING SABBATH ALONE

*What if I believe in keeping Saturday holy,
but the rest of my family doesn't?*

What a challenging opportunity! But that doesn't mean it's an easy one!

Some families who believe in keeping Saturday holy don't actually do what they believe. So I respect you for being true to your convictions. And I would think that the fourth commandment has special meaning to you. Let's look at what the first three verses of the Sabbath commandment mean.

Exodus 20:8 says: "Remember the Sabbath day by keeping it holy." The key word in this verse is remember. Evidently it's possible to forget about the Sabbath! In fact, God's people have sometimes forgotten to observe the Sabbath.

But don't let someone tell you that the Sabbath was only for the historical Jews. The word remember proves that Sabbath observance began at Creation, not on Mount Sinai (see Genesis 2:1-3).

God made the Sabbath, and He wishes for us to be part of what He considers special. It's a present from God, and who wouldn't want to "open" a present from Him?

Returning to Exodus 20, we continue by reading verse 9 and part of verse 10: "Six days you shall labor and do all your work, but the seventh day is a Sabbath to the Lord your God."

Even "holy Joes" and "holy Janes" have to work and earn a living. For teens that usually means going to school as well as holding a part-time job. Most of us are used to going to school and/or work five days a week and then having the weekend to do our own thing.

But I really believe that all our time belongs to God, and He tells us to take a break each week. Why? It helps prevent burnout, and it helps us focus on our vital relationship with Him.

The rest of verse 10 says, "On it you shall not do any work, neither you, nor your son or daughter, nor your manservant or maidservant, nor your animals, nor the alien within your gates."

Sabbath isn't just for you. It's for all humans and even animals! Parents usually share Sabbath with their children, but it sounds as if your situation is just the opposite—you share it with your family. One of these days when you have a family of your own (even if it's a one-person family), you can make Sabbath traditions.

For now, while you live in your parents' house, you have to respect their choices (notice that the next commandment deals with honoring your parents). Yet it's quite common for teens to begin doing things separately from their parents. After all, you're becoming independent.

Now let's move on to Exodus 20:11. It says, "For in six days the Lord made the heavens and the earth, the sea, and all that is in them, but he rested on the seventh day. Therefore the Lord blessed the Sabbath day and made it holy."

Did you catch the significance of this verse? It says that the Sabbath is a weekly reminder that God is God and that He made us. This fact becomes extra meaningful when we feel worthless. (Hey, get a grip! God made you, and He doesn't make junk!)

God is our original Father (Luke 3:38), and heaven was our original home (where we'll return someday). Remembering where we're *from* helps keep us focused on *where we're going.*

Now, let's talk about how these ideas apply to your situation. We know that God has reserved a special day each week to celebrate with you. Will you stiff Him? Or are you ready to take a break (rest) each week to party (celebrate) with God?

It's certainly possible to party with only God. But sometimes a party is actually more fun with a bunch of people. Hey, that's what church is about.

So if your family isn't observing Sabbath, you might get more of a Sabbath focus with your church family than with your blood family. That's what my mom did as a teen.

I had the advantage of growing up in a family that celebrated the Sabbath. So most Sabbaths were already planned for me. As a teen I just sort of cruised along and didn't make my own choices about how to celebrate Sabbath.

But it sounds as though you'll mature faster than I did in making Sabbath choices. That's great. You're deciding already what Sabbath means to you, and you're taking the responsibility to make it happen.

Keep tapping into the blessing God has for you with the Sabbath. And when your family members see what a great experience it is for you, won't they want a piece of the action?

SHOPPING ON SABBATH

Why is buying on the Sabbath wrong?

Here's your quick-fix text: "When the neighboring peoples bring merchandise or grain to sell on the Sabbath, we will not buy from them on the Sabbath or on any holy day" (Nehemiah 10:31).

Now, here's a little background to the text. God's people had faced hard consequences because of poor choices. They had lived their own way and figured that since they were God's people, bad times wouldn't come to them. Wrong!

After they tried things their own way and paid the price, they were ready to give God's way a try. So they recommitted to the things God had set out for them years before (Exodus tells all about it). That included not doing their shopping on Sabbath.

After all, market day is hardly a day of worship. While we may chuckle at the T-shirt slogan "Born to shop," it's certainly not the reason God made us!

Nehemiah 13:15-22 describes what happened after their promise. When the merchants still brought things to sell, Nehemiah told them to leave and not desecrate the Sabbath; otherwise, he would lay hands on them (see verse 21). *The Clear Word* gently paraphrases what Nehemiah said: "If they persisted and tried to come in, I would have them arrested."

Some people today pose questions involving "emergency situations," such as "If I was going to die and there was some medicine that I could buy, but it was Sabbath, should I buy it?"

Please! If Jesus condoned pulling an ox out of the ditch on Sabbath (see Matthew 12:11), certainly people should be saved, especially on Sabbath.

But don't equate that with going shopping because you just didn't get around to it during your busy week. The story of the manna (Exodus 16—the whole chapter) gives good guidance for preparing for Sabbath in advance. When you do that, there aren't as many "emergency" needs for shopping, which frees you to have quality and quantity time with your God.

WHY GO TO CHURCH?

What happens if I don't go to church?

You miss out.
Some people think the Bible tells us to go to church. Actually, I don't think there's a single Bible verse that specifically tells us that.

Luke 4:16 says that it was Jesus' "custom" to go to the synagogue each Sabbath. And Hebrews 10:25 encourages us to not give up meeting together. But the context is about persevering in our commitment to Christ. It explains that meeting with other Christians can help us keep our commitment strong.

Before you think I'm against going to church, though, let me say that going to church can be one of the best ways to keep the Sabbath. It can be the high point of the week. And it can put you in touch with God. So I'm very much in favor of going to church on Sabbath!

Granted, I'm sure most people have experienced a Sabbath they wish they hadn't gone to church. Perhaps it was a boring church service or a squabble they got into with someone. The music may have turned them off, or maybe they were appalled by who showed up!

And then teens of every generation ask, "Can't we just go to the mountains or the ocean on Sabbath instead of church?" Yes, and many youth groups actually do this as a special event.

But we miss out if we don't go to church. Part of the Sabbath experience is worshiping our Creator. Now, we can do that alone or with a group in nature. But when we join together in a sanctuary, there's a different quality about the worship experience.

I don't sing very well by myself, but when I'm with a group of praise singers and a band, things can really sound good. I can read the Bible on my own, but at church I hear about a portion of Scripture that someone has studied and now shares with me (the sermon).

I need handshakes, hugs, smiles, and good ol' friendly slaps on the back. I get those at church. I want to give those too, and church is a place where I can do that.

Many teens don't feel part of the church experience. That's when church gets boring. The remedy? Get involved. Ask your pastor and/or youth leader what you can do. If you've already got some ideas, share them with church leaders.

Don't expect everyone to completely change everything about church because you have some ideas. Other people have ideas too. But it's your church as well, so take ownership like others do.

If you're really serious, be in charge of the church service for one Sabbath. Then after you've put everything into making it a great experience, you'll be shocked if others consider it boring or wonder what would happen if they didn't come to church that Sabbath.

The answer: they'd miss out!

MY SABBATH SCHOOL IS A MESS

I'm in a small youth group of only eight to 10 people.
Many of them come from different
religious backgrounds and haven't been baptized.
The problem is that the youth always talk
among themselves while somebody's leading up front.
And whenever anyone speaks to them
about their talking, they just make snide remarks.
Is there anything I can do? Please help!
My Sabbath school's a mess.

I'm glad you're concerned about your Sabbath school, and I've got some good news for you. You can turn your youth group's negative habits into positive ones.

The fact that most teens in your group aren't baptized gives you a great opportunity to ask them where they are spiritually. Then give them a chance to answer.

Beware, though—some teens are likely to make up stuff because they think the question is too personal. To help them feel comfortable about answering honestly, don't act as if this is the great judgment day. Just make it a casual sharing experience.

After asking the teens in your group where they are spiritually, ask them where they'd like to be spiritually. Their answers are the real reasons to even have a Sabbath school or youth group.

The most common reasons for having Sabbath school and youth groups are:

• To help members start personal relationships with Jesus.

• To help members grow in their existing relationships with Jesus.

• To teach members how to let others know about Jesus.

If you discover that your youth group is meeting only out of habit or because other people are forcing you to, then no wonder everyone's acting up. If that's the case, it's time to come clean about why you guys have a youth group and why each of you attends.

Now, about all the talking that goes on in Sabbath school . . . It sounds as if the youth in your group should do more leading. (And having people from different backgrounds lead Sabbath school could add a lot of spice to your programs.)

When Sabbath school becomes a lecture session by an adult, it's common for youth to stop listening. And even if they're quiet, most youth would rather be involved.

If teens in your group aren't used to contributing to class, you may need to start gradually by breaking into smaller groups for discussions. But if they're ready to do some leading, try teaming one or two teens with an adult leader to plan and lead a Sabbath school program.

Your adult leader(s) should certainly be open to your input and leadership. In fact, the sooner your youth group members take over your own spiritual development, the better it'll be for everyone.

So go for it! Get seriously involved in your youth group, and invite the rest to join you. This is your group's chance to be real with God and with each other.

BAD SABBATH SCHOOL TEACHER

*My Sabbath school teacher is young and
doesn't interpret the Bible as he should sometimes.
He thinks he's teaching everything right, but
he's really giving his opinion; even our pastor
caught him on that. We don't know what to believe.*

Your question reminds me of the rhetorical question Pilate asked Jesus shortly before the Crucifixion: "What is truth?" (John 18:38).

When you've heard things only one way, it's quite shocking to have your viewpoint expanded by hearing from other voices—whether it's from a Sabbath school teacher, a pastor, a bright college student, or someone else's parents.

If you listen to everyone's opinions, you can get really confused. The other extreme, though, is to listen to only one person's viewpoint. Little kids often do that, but it will leave you in a very small world if that's what you do for the rest of your life—sort of like never going beyond your front yard.

So how can you know what to believe? Everyone has their own idea of what is true or right. So you need something more encompassing than just any person's own ideas.

That's where the Bible shines. It's God's messages, supernaturally given to us so we don't have to go on a bunch of human ideas.

And yes, lots of people have different ideas about the Bible! What should a person do to find the "truth" in the Bible? Here are a few suggestions from one person—me!

• **READ THE BIBLE FOR YOURSELF.** Don't just rely on

45

what others say the Bible says.

• **READ THE BIBLE IN CONTEXT.** Check the verses before and after, plus get a little idea of what was going on at the time. Some study Bibles have this information alongside the Bible verses.

• **PRAY.** Ask the God who inspired the Bible when it was written to inspire you when you read it!

• **KEEP GROWING!** While the Bible has messages that are as simple as $2 + 2 = 4$, there are also deeper discoveries to be made with more study. So keep checking it out!

• **FOCUS ON JESUS.** The purpose of the Bible is to take you to Jesus, not just to glean a few facts or bits of "truth." Ironically, the religious leaders in Jesus' day knew their Bibles very well, but they missed the Person the Bible was all about!

Jesus said it this way: "You have your heads in your Bibles constantly because you think you'll find eternal life there. But you miss the forest for the trees. These Scriptures are all about me! And here I am, standing right before you, and you aren't willing to receive from me the life you say you want" (John 5:39, 40, Message).

The Bible is an awesome source of direct truth. But you must ask the Holy Spirit to help you get the messages from the Bible. Go for it!

STICKY SPIRITUAL ISSUES

DO WE HAVE FREE WILL?

If God already knows exactly what's going to happen in our lives, then how do we really have a choice? I mean, is it really a choice if God already knows what we're going to choose?

Your question has been debated for centuries, and most Christians support one of the following two ideas.

1. GOD IS SOVEREIGN. God is God, and you're just a creature, not the Creator, so don't mess with the supernatural! Genesis 1 demonstrates that God creates without the need for human input or choice.

Scripture supports the metaphor of God as the potter and us as merely clay (Isaiah 64:8; Jeremiah 18:6; Romans 9:21). We also see this concept in the familiar song that goes: "Have thine own way, Lord! / Have thine own way! / Thou art the potter; / I am the clay. / Mold me and make me / After thy will, / While I am waiting, / Yielded and still."

2. HUMANS HAVE CHOICE. God made us in His image, which includes not only creative power but also the power of choice. The tree of the knowledge of good and evil (Genesis 2:16, 17) shows this principle at work be-

47

fore sin even entered our planet. And since the Fall, God repeatedly asks us to *choose* Him (Joshua 24:15; 1 Kings 18:21; Revelation 3:20).

Both of the above perspectives are based on the Bible, yet they seem to be opposites. If God made us in His image, and our obedience is based on love, then aren't we more than robots carrying out His "plan"? On the other hand, we obviously make choices, so do we really need God when we can do the same types of things He does (make choices, create things, etc.)?

When two seeming opposites are both true, we have a paradox. Jesus presented many paradoxes ("to be rich, give away everything you have"; "if you want to be the greatest, be the least"; "to be religious, don't copy the religious leaders," etc.).

In the same way, we have a paradox when we try to merge "God is sovereign" and "humans have choice." Can these apparent opposites both be true?

Yes. Check out the Sermon on the Mount (Matthew 5-7) and notice how both truths appear in chapter 6:

• If you forgive others (your choice), God forgives you (God's sovereignty)—verses 14, 15.

• Your heart will be in heaven if you choose (choice) to put your treasure there —verses 19-21.

• God takes care of the entire earth (God's sovereignty), so you don't need to worry about yourself (choice)—verses 25-32.

• Make God's kingdom number one in your life (choice), and God will take care of everything else (God's sovereignty)—verse 33.

So how do we deal with this paradox of God's sovereignty and human choice? Because God is in control, make your choices wisely!

FAITH OR WORKS?

*Does it take both faith and works
to get us to heaven, or just faith?*

The typical answer is "Just faith, *but* you've got to have works, too!" That's downright confusing.

The correct answer is *neither*. Faith won't get you to heaven, and neither will works. Honest! What gets you to heaven is *grace*.

Someone has turned that word into an acronym: **G**od's **R**iches **A**t **C**hrist's **E**xpense. I just say it's a gift from God.

The Bible tells it this way: "For by *grace* you have been saved through faith; and this is not your own doing, it is the gift of God" (Ephesians 2:8, RSV).

It's hard to accept gifts. We think that people give us gifts because of what we've already done, or else, if their gifts are more than we deserve, we feel as if we owe them something. We like to take the text above and emphasize "through faith," as though our part—believing that God gave us the gift—is more important than God's part—the gift itself.

Why not just admit that salvation is *completely* a gift from God to us? Take it or leave it, but don't dwell on our relatively insignificant part in making salvation happen.

What about the works part? Keep reading Ephesians 2. In verse 10 God tells us that He already made provision for us to do good works. It's not a payment to earn the gift. It's part of the gift!

WHY ARE THERE SO MANY CATCHES?

*If all we have to do is believe to be saved,
then why are there so many catches?*

Most people want to live forever. That's why Jesus' offer of eternal life leads us to ask the obvious question—what does it take?

This was the rich young ruler's first question when he encountered Jesus. "Good teacher, what must I do to inherit eternal life?" (Luke 18:18).

Jesus' answer surprises many today, because it smacks of legalism. "You know the commandments: 'Do not commit adultery, do not murder, do not steal, do not give false testimony, honor your father and mother.'"

Following these commandments certainly could be considered virtuous. Yet my college pastor used to say, "The Ten Commandments might make you a good liver, but that's not enough."

I think he's right. Being a "good liver" has its benefits, but it's not your ticket to heaven.

In fact, the rich young ruler claimed to have an impeccable commandment-keeping record—"'All these I have kept since I was a boy,' he said" (verse 21).

His claim makes you wonder if he'd deluded himself into believing that he really had obeyed all God's commandments since he was a kid. Yet the poor guy still didn't have assurance of eternal security.

Sensing the young man's frustration, Jesus offered him the missing piece of the puzzle. "You still lack one thing," Jesus said.

Yes, the young man had sensed that! What was the one thing? Of course he'd do it! He wanted to live forever.

"Sell everything you have and give to the poor. . . . Then come, follow me" (verse 22).

How's that for a challenge? It goes way beyond just believing, doesn't it? And it certainly exceeds the Ten Commandments, doesn't it?

The Ten Commandments might be difficult to really follow all the time, but at least they aren't ridiculous! the young ruler must have thought. *Imagine selling all my riches! I thought You said I just needed to keep the commandments.*

Jesus exposed how superficially this guy was keeping the commandments. For when Jesus challenged him on the first one—"You shall have no other gods besides me" (Exodus 20:3)—the guy who'd supposedly obeyed God's commandments since childhood failed.

The Ten Commandments do provide helpful guidance for living a good life, but they don't provide eternal life. They do expose the fact that we don't do everything right, and that's why we need Jesus to save us.

Now let's take the idea that all we need to do is "believe" in Him to be saved. Lots of people claim to believe, but when it comes to living out their belief, they do squat.

The apostle James put it this way: "Are there still some among you who hold that 'only believing' is enough? . . . . Fool! When will you ever learn that 'believing' is useless without doing what God wants you to? Faith that does not result in good deeds is not real faith" (James 2:19, 20, TLB).

Suppose someone cool of the opposite sex says to you, "I'd like for us to be much more than just friends." Your heart flutters, and your face flushes. The person continues, "How much time do I have to spend with you for us to be considered boyfriend and girlfriend?"

Such a calculating and callous question might make your face flush even more, but for a different reason!

Simply "doing the right thing" isn't enough, is it?

Some people, such as the rich young ruler, like the idea of living forever. But the reason Jesus wants to give us eternal life is so that we can live forever *with Him.*

If that kind of a living arrangement doesn't appeal to you (and if God's commandments seem full of catches), you need something more than a die-free body. You need a new heart.

Jesus willingly offers it to you: "I will give you a new heart—I will give you new and right desires—and put a new spirit within you. I will take out your stony hearts of sin and give you new hearts of love" (Ezekiel 36:26, TLB).

According to 1 John 5:3, "the proof that we love God comes when we keep his commandments and they are not at all troublesome" (Message).

That makes sense only when we receive a new heart of love from God. And that happens when we put all our trust and belief in Him (that's what the rich young ruler failed to do).

Without putting our trust in God, the Ten Commandments might seem like a bunch of catches. But God doesn't play games. He doesn't offer us eternal life and then hound us with nitpicking rules. He wants to make us new creations!

In Romans 2:4 Paul says, "God is kind, but he's not soft. In kindness he takes us firmly by the hand and leads us into a radical life change" (Message).

For those who want eternal life, that means a radical life change now—one that'll last forever.

CAN WE ABUSE FORGIVENESS?

Are we able to abuse forgiveness?

Yes. I do it all the time. I'm not proud about that. In fact, it's quite humiliating when I stop to think about it.

But that might be the problem—I rarely think about it. In Old Testament times, people had to take a lamb to the Temple and actually kill it as part of the forgiveness process (and we think we have it bad). It had to be one of their best lambs.

That would make you think twice before casually doing something wrong. But the Israelites actually got to the point that sacrificing animals became a thoughtless ritual. According to Isaiah 1, God was sick of the animal sacrifices the people brought. He wanted to forgive and purify them inside their minds and hearts.

Now we don't sacrifice animals as part of our forgiveness process, because God sent the Sacrifice of all time to die for us. Even though we weren't there, in effect we killed a person, not an animal. Even more extreme, we killed God! When the reality of that hits us, then the forgiveness God offers overwhelms us. Appreciating this pretty much destroys a carefree attitude toward forgiveness.

Perhaps we abuse forgiveness the most when we don't pass it on to others. You'll find the story of a forgiveness abuser in Matthew 18:23-35. If you haven't received God's forgiveness, you won't have much to pass on to others (and you won't be much fun to be around, either). When we really accept the forgiveness God offers us, instead of getting mad at piddley things others do to us, we pass on a small portion of the forgiveness we've received.

Some think that God won't forgive them if they abuse His forgiveness, especially if they did something wrong on purpose. *Wrong!* God actually describes Himself as full of mercy and compassion, gracious and kind, overflowing with love and forgiveness (see Exodus 34:6).

The biggest abuse of forgiveness is not to accept it when God died for us so we can receive it. It's all yours because of Him.

WHO'S LUCIFER?

Who's Lucifer, and where did he come from?

The name Lucifer appears only once in the whole Bible (in Isaiah 14:12). In the New King James Version it reads, "How you are fallen from heaven, O Lucifer, son of the morning! How you are cut down to the ground, you who weakened the nations!"

If you look back to verse 4, you'll see that technically these comments were written about the king of Babylon. But most readers recognize that some of these characteristics seem more like Satan. In fact, many times the king of Babylon acted very much like Satan. And when he did, what was said about Satan applied to the wicked king as well.

Jesus made a similar connection when talking to some of the leaders of His day. He pointed out that God wasn't their Father, because they weren't acting like children of God. He told them, "You belong to your father, the devil, and you want to carry out your father's desire. He was a murderer from the beginning. . . . When he lies, he speaks his native language, for he is a liar and the father of lies" (John 8:44).

The name Lucifer actually means "shining or brilliant one." The Latin word Lucifer means "light bearer." If you have the NIV translation of the Bible, Isaiah 14:12 uses the expression "morning star," which refers to Venus, the brightest star. Lucifer was the creature (angel) that was brighter than all the others God made.

You can link Isaiah 14:12 with similar passages, such as Ezekiel 28:12-17, which deals with the king of Tyre but makes obvious reference to Satan, too. Another reference is Revelation 12:7-9.

Where did Lucifer come from? From God. One of the most perplexing questions is how the highest created being (made "perfect") could start the whole sin problem. Since God takes ultimate responsibility for Satan (and for sin), He has taken the initiative for all who sin to be saved.

Satan and his followers consistently choose not to be saved. How tragic. And some people on earth today make the same choices—equally tragic!

Since God is ultimately responsible, God will eventually bring the entire sin thing to an end. The good news is that all of us have many opportunities to choose God instead of sin. What have you been choosing lately?

WHY DID GOD CREATE SATAN?

Why didn't God just not create Satan and his angels?

Hey, I hear you! If I were God, I wouldn't create anybody who didn't tow the line. There'd be nobody disobeying me in my kingdom.

Of course, nobody has ever volunteered to be in my kingdom. So the only way I could get them there would be to force them. And then I'd stay busy trying to keep them there!

If you look at some of the governments that oppress people, you'll get an idea of how I'd run this planet. It's a good thing I'm not God!

Thinking about Satan and his angels, though, here's the part that blows me away: all the angels had a chance to choose whether they'd stay with God in His kingdom—or leave with Satan. Remarkably, 30 percent chose to leave! (See Revelation 12:3, 4, 9.) Now, that's what I call a bad choice! Satan must have been very convincing back then, just as he is today!

If you want a more detailed answer to your question, I recommend you read the first chapter of *Patriarchs and Prophets,* by Ellen White. It's about 10 pages long and is called "Why Was Sin Permitted?"

If you don't have the book, just ask your pastor if you can borrow a copy. And if you can't get ahold of a copy, let me know!

Now, while God always gives people free choice in His kingdom, Satan rules his kingdom by the law of the jungle: "Might equals right." This method of government works only while "might" is exercised and people feel threatened.

Throughout history human governments have tried to impose this "might equals right" way. And millions have died as a result of forceful dictators.

Yet an interesting thing happens. Those who die as martyrs and "rebels" often inspire those left alive not to give in to "might equals right."

I'm glad force isn't God's way. He wins followers by love instead of "knuckles and fists."

Of course, because Adam and Eve (who had free choice) chose to sin, we've inherited from them a sinful nature. And when we give in to sin and Satan's control, we lose our power.

Yet when Jesus died for us, He restored to us our chance to make an eternal choice—a choice that boils down to one question: Will you live for yourself, or will you live for Jesus, your Creator and Saviour?

Isn't God amazing? You can choose whether or not to accept God's gift of eternal life and be in His kingdom. He lets you decide!

Now here's another question for you to think about: Why didn't God just not create you?

WHAT ABOUT WOMEN MINISTERS?

*Is there anything that prevents women
from being ministers?*

Because males have functioned as pastors for so long and females have functioned in assistant or associate roles, many women may not have even considered this an option. (In the same way females years ago didn't picture themselves as physicians, but nurses.)

But the crucial issue regarding whether or not you're a minister is whether or not God equips you to minister. If God does, then there's no reason you can't minister. You may not get the position you'd like, but that doesn't need to stop you from ministering where you are. (Most males don't get the position they want either!)

Actually, there's a shortage of pastors in North America at this time. One conference official recently reported an estimated 200 pastoral positions available. And some conferences are especially seeking female pastors. But other conferences still shy away from hiring females.

In the Northern California Conference in the year 2000, there were more than 100 pastors. Only one was female. I asked her to answer your question, because I've found that females often have a vital perspective that males just don't have. So here's her response:

"My name is Marit, and I've been an associate pastor at the Pacific Union College church for more than eight years. I really enjoy my job, and my congregation is supportive and accepting of me.

"I don't think there's anything that prevents women from being ministers. In fact, I would encourage women to become ministers! And since 60 percent of most church memberships are made up of women, I think that as a woman you can minister to this group in a unique and different way.

"When I first arrived on this campus, many women told me they were so glad I was here. Why? Because women relate differently to a woman pastor—somebody who understands what it means to be a woman in today's society; somebody who looks at the Bible through the eyes of a woman; somebody they can spend one-on-one time with without having to be afraid of sexual implications.

"Right now ordination isn't something that's been approved for women ministers in the Seventh-day Adventist denomination. So if you're looking to become an ordained minister, you might have to think twice.

"But I'm finding that I function and participate in church life the same way my ordained colleagues do. In fact, baby dedications and baptisms are my specialties!

"I feel honored and blessed by the opportunities God has provided for me to serve and be a part of my congregation."

I thought that was a good answer. (In fact, I thought it was such a good answer that I proposed to that woman, and she's now my wife!)

SILENT IN CHURCH?

*I'm a little confused about what 1 Corinthians 14:34, 35
says. Should women remain silent in church?
Does God think it's wrong for a female to be
a pastor or evangelist? Would God think I
was bad if I were to stand before the church
and give a testimony or something?*

Those verses in 1 Corinthians 14 do seem to plainly
oppose women speaking in church. But three
chapters earlier, in 1 Corinthians 11:5, Paul wrote that
every woman who prays or prophesies needs to follow the custom in the churches at that time and cover
her head.

If women were never to utter a word in church, why
did Paul bother to tell them to cover their heads when
praying or prophesying? He should have told them to
cover their mouths instead of their heads if he really
didn't want them to speak in church!

Now, to understand those verses in 1 Corinthians
14, we must read the entire chapter. Then we discover
that Paul was talking about orderly worship.

Because of the way the church members in Corinth
were using the gift of tongues, things were getting
pretty rowdy during their church services. That's why
Paul gave them practical counsel about how to have orderly worship in church.

As part of his message, he mentioned that women
are to "remain silent" (verse 34). You'll find that same
kind of language in verses 28 and 30.

But notice how all three verses relate to orderly
worship services.

In verse 28 Paul said that if someone wants to speak in tongues but there isn't anyone present to interpret the message, the person should "keep quiet" instead of speaking in an unknown language.

In verse 30 he advised that if a person is sharing a prophecy and somebody else receives an additional prophecy during the church service, the first person should "stop" to let the second message come through.

Keep in mind that the church in Corinth probably followed the same custom as the Jewish synagogue. That meant that the men sat on one side, and the women sat on the other side.

So Paul advised in verse 35 that if a woman had a question about something being said in church, instead of shouting across the church to her husband, she should "remain silent" and ask him about it at home.

Imagine a church service in which people are speaking different languages all at the same time. Then several people claim to have just received messages from God, so they grab microphones and all start talking at once. Then Gertrude shouts across the church to her husband, "Harry, what did that guy say?" Talk about chaos!

So this passage isn't about prohibiting women from giving a testimony, a sermon, a lesson study, or a prayer for the congregation. It's about orderly worship.

If God's given you a message, definitely share it with the rest of the church. Just do it in an orderly manner.

ELLEN WHITE ABOVE THE BIBLE?

Why do so many Seventh-day Adventists put the writings of Ellen White before or next to the Bible?

B ecause they want someone to tell them specifically what to do instead of wrestling with what God has already explained in the Bible.

Ever since sin separated us from Him, God has found various ways to communicate to us. Hebrews 1:1, 2 explains, "Long ago God spoke to our ancestors in many and various ways by the prophets, but in these last days he has spoken to us by a Son" (NRSV).

The Old Testament gave some great insights because it recorded God's messages through the prophets. But when Jesus came, since He was God, He gave God's messages directly.

I'm thankful so much was written down for our use in the New Testament! We have the entire Bible to get messages from God. Seventh-day Adventists believe the Bible is God's special message for all time.

But God still communicates to us in other ways in addition to the Bible. Hopefully God sends you messages through sermons your preacher delivers. Maybe He has given other people words of encouragement through you!

According to Joel 2:28, 29 (repeated in Acts 2:17, 18), God will send lots of messages through a variety of people—young and old, male and female, those who seem important and those who don't. We shouldn't be surprised that God sent messages to a small group of Adventists through someone named Ellen White. We should be surprised if we don't see and hear from a lot more messengers!

Some religions think that the latest word is the best word. Whatever the latest prophet says supersedes anything before it.

Seventh-day Adventists believe that the Bible supersedes everything else. For Adventists, any "recent messages" must be checked against the standard—the Bible.

You can see why it's crucial that we're familiar with the Bible. If that's our standard, we need to know what it says, or our standard becomes a joke.

There's no doubt that many people have received inspiring messages from God when they read something out of *Steps to Christ* or *The Desire of Ages.* If you haven't read a chapter or two from one of those books recently, I highly recommend it.

Yet some have misused advice written to specific individuals by implying that those testimonies should apply to everybody. That would be like taking a letter you wrote to a group of friends, perhaps including an invitation to come to your house one evening, and then suggesting that the letter, including the invitation, is for everybody.

The purpose of the Bible (and any messages from other prophets) is to express God's communication to us. Consider this an invitation to invest some time reading what God has already communicated.

While we as a church place Ellen White's writings in a prophetic category, we officially state that we believe "the Bible is the standard by which all teaching and experience must be tested" (*Seventh-day Adventists Believe,* p. 216; see also pp. 227 and 228).

In spite of these official beliefs, here are a few reasons some Seventh-day Adventists seem to place Ellen White's writings higher than the Bible.

• They don't believe—as do true Seventh-day Adventists—that the Bible really is number one.

• The writings of Ellen White total more pages than

the Bible, so people think they're more likely to find something in her work to prove their point—or to instruct or disprove someone else.

• Because Ellen White wrote 100 years ago instead of 2,000 years ago, some people think her writings seem more relevant for our time—the last days.

• Because they've gotten messages from God through Ellen White's writings in the past, some people keep referring back to them for more messages.

Many people who misuse Ellen White's writings aren't even aware they're doing it. So here's a suggestion: if someone you know seems to put Ellen White's writings higher than the Bible, ask them to share with you what they've found most helpful about her writings.

After you've listened (and if they're ready to start listening to you), ask them when they think Joel 2:27, 28 will be fulfilled, and whether or not they think you and/or they will be part of that.

I expect God to follow through on His promise to get out many more messages shortly before He returns. So are you ready to pass along messages from God to others? Be listening for His voice!

I'M CONFUSED ABOUT TITHING

*At a recent Bible study group we couldn't come
up with a clear meaning for Leviticus 27:31
and what it says about tithing. One person said
that the texts means that if you use your tithe
for something else and then pay it back to God
a week later, you need to add one fifth more to
the amount. Is that what Leviticus 27:31 is saying?*

First, I want to commend you for participating in a
Bible study group. It's a great way to grow in your
love for God and fellowship with others who are seeking Him too.

In the King James Version Leviticus 27:31 reads:
"And if a man will at all redeem ought of his tithes, he
shall add thereto the fifth part thereof."

If I had been in your Bible study group and heard
that text, I probably would have said, "What?" Then I
would have asked if someone had a different translation that might be easier for me to understand.

Here's how Leviticus 27:31 reads in the New
International Version: "If a man redeems any of his
tithe, he must add a fifth of the value to it."

That sounds more like the conclusion the person in
your group came to—adding a fifth to one's tithe. But it
still might leave me wondering what it means to "redeem" any of one's tithe.

In *The Living Bible* the verse reads: "If anyone
wants to buy back this fruit or grain, he must add a
fifth to its value."

This sounds a little more like the English I speak.
Yet I want to check it out more.

So I take out my Strong's Concordance, look up the

word "redeem" in Leviticus 27:31, and find the number 1350 next to it. In the back of the concordance in the Hebrew (Old Testament) dictionary section, I look up word number 1350. The definition reads: "to purchase, ransom or redeem."

Still not quite sure what the verse means, I read the verse before it (Leviticus 27:30), which talks about tithing harvested food. Then I read the verse after it, which talks about tithing flocks and other livestock.

Because I'm not a farmer or rancher like many people who lived in Bible times, this concept isn't familiar to me. So I reach for my seven-volume *Seventh-day Adventist Bible Commentary* set published by the Review and Herald Publishing Association. These books give a verse-by-verse description of the Bible, but some verses have more explanation than others.

Here's what *The Seventh-day Adventist Bible Commentary* says about Leviticus 27:31: "The question has been raised whether it is legitimate now to withhold the tithe if later a fifth is added to it. [That sounds very much like your question, doesn't it?] This question reveals a misunderstanding of the words of Scripture. It was not a matter of withholding tithe that demanded a fifth to be added. It was a question of paying the tithe in kind, in wheat, barley, or whatever produce was tithed. There might be cases in which a man needed wheat for sowing, and would rather pay in money than in wheat. Under these conditions he might redeem the tithe by having the wheat appraised and paying this sum plus one fifth. The withholding of tithe was never contemplated. As noted above, it was only grain and garden produce that could thus be redeemed. Cattle could not be redeemed or exchanged" (*The Seventh-day Adventist Bible Commentary,* vol. 1, p. 818).

So Leviticus 27:31 isn't about getting a loan from God and then paying Him 20 percent in penalties and interest. God already owns everything. Giving tithe is just one way to remind us that everything we have and receive comes from Him.

From what we've just read, God had a common-sense approach for farmers who needed to use part of their produce to continue their farming, yet still acknowledge their dependence on God.

You might talk to your Bible study group about dealing with another passage about tithing—Deuteronomy 12:4-7. Read from different Bible translations. Use a concordance and a commentary. Pray through the study as a group. And keep growing toward God!

WHAT HAPPENS WHEN WE DIE?

My friend once said to me that when righteous people die, they go to heaven. So I said, "If righteous people go to heaven when they die, why would Christ need to come back to take us to heaven?" Does that sound dumb?

No, it doesn't sound dumb to me. But that might be because I believe the same way you do about what happens when a person dies.

Most Christians grow up believing that when you die you go to heaven. And they never even question it. It's sort of like growing up believing that Sunday is the Sabbath. They just don't consider it any other way.

At one gathering of about 4,000 youth leaders from various denominations, a respected Baptist minister shocked the crowd when he made a statement. He said that the belief that people go to heaven when they die is just Greek cultural thought—it's not biblical. I agree.

If people were to go to heaven right after they die,

what would they be like? Would righteous souls be like Casper the friendly ghost, just floating around? Or maybe they'd be stuck on clouds playing harps.

Some people believe that the dead go to heaven, then start functioning as angels to carry out God's plans. Or they act as ambassadors for humans who hope to get God's attention. (As if God isn't interested enough in us already—how twisted!)

But if this were true, then when Jesus returns to earth, what will all these ghosts do? I guess they'll have to come back to earth and get bodies!

And if it's better to have a body instead of being a ghost, maybe heaven won't be that great until after the Second Coming. Then again, if it's better to be a ghost, the rest of eternity will be second best compared to being a ghost.

Of course, the Bible doesn't suggest these things. The serpent's promise to Eve, "You will not surely die" (Genesis 3:4), is one of the oldest lies on record. Yes, humans die. But the good news is that believers already have eternal life based on trusting Jesus (see John 5:24 and 1 John 5:11-13).

So for believers, what others think of as "death" is merely "sleep." Read the story of Lazarus in John 11 to understand the way Jesus views death.

Christ's return to take all His people home will be the biggest celebration this universe will witness. For a nice straightforward overview of what will happen when Christ returns, read 1 Thessalonians 4:15-18. (I recommend reading it from the New Living Translation.)

Did Jesus Have Girl Problems?

Did Jesus as a teen have guy/girl problems?

QUICK ANSWER: Yes. (See Matthew 32:4-10. No, that passage of Scripture doesn't exist!)

BETTER ANSWER: Jesus' teen years are condensed into one verse in the Bible (Luke 2:52). The basic message is that even though Jesus was God's Son, He was normal, which means He probably had guy/girl problems (that is normal!).

But in Jesus' day people didn't date like we do today. It was common to have a marriage arranged by the time you were about 15 years old—shocker! So Jesus stayed single after everyone else had already gotten married. Can you imagine the rumors?

If Jesus was tempted in all the ways we are, He experienced some challenges when it came to guy/girl problems. One of the big guy/girl problems Jesus had was His practice of sticking up for females rather than using them or letting others use them. The girls liked it, but the guys got ticked off—a power issue! So He had some pretty tough times in addition to the regular guy/girl problems we face.

Then add to that the basic problem of relating to all people when nobody knew who His real father was (see John 9:29; Luke 4:22; and John 8:41, where the religious leaders insinuate that Jesus is a true bastard). If you were in His shoes, how would you explain to people that your dad is actually God?

The bottom line: Jesus understands our situation, even though we rarely understand His.

SPEAKING IN TONGUES

I used to go to a Pentecostal church. During one service everyone was in a big circle holding hands and screaming in tongues (words nobody understood, but they said it was the language of heaven). I got scared and ran out and cried. When I told my mother about it, she said, "If you got scared in that church, God was probably telling you that you shouldn't go there." Do you agree?

No, but here's what I don't agree with: selecting a church based on whether or not it makes you feel good. I've heard people say, "I won't go to that particular church because I just don't feel comfortable there."

But the purpose of going to church is to worship God. And being part of a church means more than attending the church service. There arc ministries and fellowships that take place beyond the worship service.

As you become involved in a church, you might get a word from the Lord about changes you need to make in your life. Would you be open to that—or would that make you uncomfortable?

As you can tell, I react pretty strongly to the idea of a person's religion being merely comfortable.

Now, I'm not suggesting that if things are miserable, that makes them spiritual. I'm simply stating that just because a person likes something doesn't make it right or godly. It's better to have our tastes become more like God's tastes than to try to make God's tastes more like ours.

Now let's talk about the other part of your question—speaking in tongues. The term "speaking in tongues" refers to two kinds of things.

The first kinds involves being able to speak (or interpret) a language you haven't known before. In Acts 2:1-8 it's clear that on the day of Pentecost people from many language groups heard the good news about Jesus in their own language. As a result, many of them accepted Jesus as their Saviour (Acts 2:41).

So the purpose of speaking in tongues is to spread the gospel to others by being able to communicate to them in a language they understand.

But the kind of speaking in tongues most Pentecostals seek is what they claim to be a language of heaven.

Some people see 1 Corinthians 14:2 as a text that endorses a mysterious language that nobody understands. But in 1 Corinthians 14:19 Paul states that he'd rather speak five words worshipers could understand than 10,000 words they couldn't understand.

Some Pentecostals used to stress that everyone needed to speak in tongues. They claimed that was the best evidence that the Holy Spirit was in a person.

But some Pentecostal churches don't emphasize that as much anymore, especially as they've understood that the Holy Spirit gives whatever gift(s) the Spirit decides (1 Corinthians 12:11). And because the Holy Spirit doesn't give everyone the same gift, not everyone who has the Spirit will have the gift of speaking in tongues (verses 8-11, 27-31).

But some people who claim to speak in tongues are very moved by that experience and don't want to give it up, even if it's something they make up or work themselves up to do.

Personally, I've never spoken in tongues (although I've asked God to give me the gift of speaking Spanish during many mission trips to Central America!). So I can't say what it's like or what it's not like based on my experience.

But from what the Bible says I believe there's a spiritual gift of speaking a language that can lead others to Christ. I also understand, though, that it's a gift the Spirit gives to whomever the Spirit decides.

When the Spirit does give gifts to people, those people can be tempted to think they're better than everyone else because they have special abilities that come from God. But that kind of showing off makes it obvious that the people don't remember where the gift came from or what its purpose is.

So, should you go to the Pentecostal church? I encourage you to make your decision based on Bible principles we've talked about and not on feelings.

I'd also like to invite you to attend a Seventh-day Adventist church. Depending on where you live, the nearest Seventh-day Adventist church might be small, medium, or large. But I can assure you that you won't get scared there. And you can worship God with other believers who make Him number one in their lives and are committed to living for Jesus as they eagerly anticipate His return.

Many people have joined the Seventh-day Adventist Church because the beliefs and message are Bible based and make so much sense. Also, they've joined because they felt convicted by the Holy Spirit that God wanted them there.

As for me, I've found that the sooner you get involved in the Seventh-day Adventist Church, the better it is. So shall I look for you next Sabbath?

Is There a Secret Rapture?

I have some friends who believe in the rapture. But I know that as Seventh-day Adventists we believe in the second coming of Christ. I don't know which scriptures support our teaching, though. And my friends seem to believe in the Bible too. So which texts can I use to prove the Second Coming rather than the secret rapture?

As Seventh-day Adventists we look to the Bible for our beliefs. And it sounds as if you want to do that too.

But people can prove almost anything using just one "proof" text—especially when they take it out of context. So be sure to read texts in context (consider what the verses before and after the text say).

And don't build a major belief on just one text. If it's a major belief to God, you can expect to read about it in more than one place in the Bible.

Now, this might surprise you, but I actually believe in the rapture! Why? Because the Bible says it will happen. The Bible also explains how it will happen.

The word "rapture" is found in only one passage: 1 Thessalonians 4:16, 17. It reads, "For the Lord himself will come down from heaven, with a loud command, with the voice of the archangel and with the trumpet call of God, and the dead in Christ will rise first. After that, we who are still alive and are left will be caught up together with them in the clouds to meet the Lord in the air. And so we will be with the Lord forever."

The phrase "caught up" is the translation of the Latin word for "rapture." While I believe in the rapture because it's mentioned in the Bible, I certainly don't believe that it will be "secret." How can it be secret when it's going to be preceded by a loud command, the voice of an archangel, and the trumpet call of God?

But let's see how this belief came about in the first place. About 500 years ago people were accusing a church leader of being the antichrist. So one church scholar named Franciscos Ribera came up with a plan to divert attention from the accusation. He started teaching that Daniel's 70-week prophecy (see Daniel 9) would end with a seven-year period of tribulation sometime in the future. And that's when the antichrist would be revealed.

Later (about 100 years ago) a lawyer named John Darby added the concept of dispensations (different chapters in the history of the world). He taught that at the end of the world (during the last week of Daniel's 70-week prophecy), Christ's church would be secretly "raptured" away to heaven. Then the Jews, who had to remain on earth, would get their chapter in history, a final time of tribulation in which to choose Christ.

That led to Cyrus Scofield including ideas about the secret rapture in his notes in *The Scofield Reference Bible,* which he published in 1909. People reading his notes began to accept his comments as part of Scripture.

Then in the 1970s Hal Lindsey published a best-selling book called *The Late Great Planet Earth.* In it he popularized the secret rapture by showing it as an attractive way for the world to end—God's people getting raptured from this earth before the time of tribulation.

Nowadays many Christian theologians, authors, and professors believe in the secret rapture—followed by seven years of tribulation, followed by Christ's visible second coming. But while it sounds comfortable to be raptured and not have to go through any time of trouble, this theory just doesn't fit with what the rest of the Bible says.

Besides, Jesus Himself told His disciples, "In this world you will have trouble. But take heart! I have overcome the world" (John 16:33).

Remember, God didn't rapture Shadrach, Meshach, and Abednego before they were thrown into the fiery furnace. Nor did He rapture Daniel before he was sent into a lions' den. Why, then, would God change His process and rapture us before the time of trouble?

Modern Christians still face very difficult situations. But like Shadrach, Meshach, Abednego, and Daniel, they usually come through them even more dependent on Jesus. (See 2 Corinthians 12:7-10.)

I've also found that many people who believe in a secret rapture are paranoid that they might not get raptured anyway. They fear that then they'll be on their own for a seven-year time of trouble.

But that's not what Jesus told his disciples either. He promised that He'd be with His followers "to the very end of the age" (Matthew 28:20).

The secret rapture theory contains another dangerous idea. It implies that if you miss the rapture, you can go to heaven seven years later, when Jesus comes the "second" time.

But Jesus never suggests that anyone can wait for the future to hook into spiritual things. The message is always "Do it today!" (See Hebrews 4:7, which quotes Psalm 95:7, 8. See also 2 Corinthians 6:1, 2.)

For some texts about the Second Coming, why not check out Matthew 24, Mark 13, and Luke 21, to see what Jesus said about it. Also, Jesus' disciple John wrote Revelation, an entire book about the Second Coming! John 14-17 also gives some good guidance about how we should live as we anticipate Christ's return. So do Jesus' three parables in Matthew 25.

The only passage someone might think supports the secret rapture is Matthew 24:40, 41. Those verses talk about one man being "taken and the other left."

But if you look at verses 37-39, you'll see that this

passage is actually saying that some people will be surprised when Jesus returns. For example, in the days of Noah the Flood surprised some people (even though Noah had built the ark and preached about the flood for 100 years) and "took them all away."

The Flood didn't "rapture" those people—it "took them away" (they died). And the same thing will happen when Jesus returns. Some people will be taken away—they'll die. And others will be raptured the way 1 Thessalonians 4:17 states—it will be no secret!

So the secret rapture theory isn't supported in the Bible. The Bible does say that Jesus is coming, but not secretly. And before He comes, if we face trouble, He'll be with us and help us through it.

In the meantime, let's take Jesus' advice: "Do not let your hearts be troubled and do not be afraid" (John 14:27).

WHAT WILL WE DO IN HEAVEN?

After we get to heaven, what will we do there?
Are we going to be able to play sports, watch TV,
and listen to our favorite music on the radio?
Will our pets be there? Will we have jobs?
Will we be immortal? What will our purpose be?
Are we just going to float on clouds and play harps?

Great questions! I can answer a few of them with pretty straightforward answers. For the others I'll have to use a "sanctified imagination."

When my daughter was 5 years old, she announced that she knew what heaven will be like. Pleasantly surprised, I asked her to describe it.

"The first floor is a giant swimming pool—the

biggest one you've ever seen," she began. "The second floor is the world's biggest Toys Я Us store. The third floor is a giant Discovery Zone [indoor playground and games]. The fourth floor is another huge swimming pool [we had been doing a lot of swimming that spring]. And the fifth floor is the biggest Carl's Junior [her favorite fast food joint at the time, primarily because of its play area]."

Obviously, my daughter was thinking of the things she liked best in life. And she figured if she could put them all together, that would be heaven for her!

But since the Bible is our authority, let's use it to find out more about heaven.

Isaiah 65 records many of the promises God made to the children of Israel (which were never fulfilled, but many Christians believe that they will be in heaven). Verse 25 says, "The wolf and the lamb will feed together, and the lion will eat straw like the ox." That's the verse that has led to paintings of heaven depicting children petting lions while standing next to lambs.

As far as pets are concerned, the Bible doesn't say whether or not they'll be in heaven. I've heard the popular answer that goes something like this: "Since God wants the best for us, and since we loved our pets (assuming we did), God will restore them to us in heaven." That answer sounds nice to me, but the Bible doesn't hint one way or the other.

When it comes to harps, most of the biblical references are in the Old Testament. The harp was a common musical instrument used both to worship God (Psalm 150:3) and to worship idols (Daniel 3:5). Today we might refer to guitars the same way.

Revelation 5:12, 13 tells us that there will be music in heaven. And harps are mentioned three times in Revelation—5:8, 14:2, and 15:2 (though those verses say nothing about clouds or halos). The last part of

Revelation 15:2 reads, "They held harps given them by God and sang the song of Moses the servant of God and the song of the Lamb."

It's pretty obvious that verse mentions harps. Yet with all the symbols in Revelation, I wouldn't say yes or no to actual harps. But I'm looking forward to singing the song of Moses and the Lamb (the song of victory)! In fact, I'm looking forward to just singing without bothering other people!

Will we be immortal? *Yes,* finally. We aren't now, even though many Christians mistakenly think that when a person dies, that person's spirit goes on living. That's a Greek idea, not a biblical one. First Timothy 6:15, 16 makes it clear that only God is immortal, and He will give us the gift of immortality when Jesus returns and destroys death (see 1 Corinthians 15:50-55).

What will be our purpose in heaven? I believe it will be the same as it is now—*to glorify God.* Check out Matthew 5:16; John 15:8; Romans 15:6; 1 Corinthians 6:20 and 10:31; Revelation 5; Revelation 7:9-17; Revelation 14:6, 7; and Revelation 19:1-7.

We often think that happiness is the ultimate achievement. But happiness is a by-product, not a goal. In fact, if happiness becomes our goal, we're almost certain not to reach it! I'm still looking for the text that says what I've heard preachers say: "God just wants you to be happy." Sorry, that's not what life's all about.

Try this. Meditate on Revelation 21:1 through 22:7 and 2 Peter 3:9-14. These verses talk about everything being new, no more tears or crying, a river of life, the visible presence of God, and more.

Ask God to fill your mind with possibilities for what heaven will be like. After all, He's promised to give us some clues—see 1 Corinthians 2:9, 10!

What's Wrong With ... ?

Dancing

I'm starting high school this year, and my mom doesn't want me to go to any dances. Is dancing OK for an Adventist? If it's not, why not? And if it is, what makes it that way? Also, how can I get my parents to say it's OK, or to think I'm responsible enough to handle this?

Before I respond to your specific questions, let me address a bigger issue—the importance of keeping open, respectful communication between you and your parents. Instead of pitting yourself against them, ask them if you can discuss the topic of dancing with them. Then ask for their input and instruction. Be sure also to ask them how they dealt with similar things when they were your age and how other people dealt with them too. Then ask them to listen to your perspective. And share not just information, but also your feelings.

When you can do this, you and your parents will be on the same team, even though you won't necessarily agree on everything. If you can't do this, most things, even trivial things, could become major battles.

As you discuss this topic with your parents, I recommend looking up all the verses in the Bible about dancing. There aren't that many—only 27. While other biblical principles might relate to dancing without using that exact word, at least check out the passages that mention the word "dance." Here are the texts (from the King James Version):

DANCE	DANCING
Judges 21:21	Exodus 32:19
Job 21:1	1 Samuel 18:6
Psalm 149:3	1 Samuel 30:16
Psalm 150:4	2 Samuel 6:16
Ecclesiastes 3:4	1 Chronicles 15:29
Isaiah 13:21	Psalm 30:11
Jeremiah 31:13	Luke 15:25
Lamentations 5:15	

DANCES	DANCED
Exodus 15:20	Judges 21:23
Judges 11:34	2 Samuel 6:14
Judges 21:21	Matthew 11:17
1 Samuel 21:11	Matthew 14:6
1 Samuel 29:5	Mark 6:22
Jeremiah 31:4	Luke 7:32

Obviously, not all dances are the same. Do some analysis. Which passages refer to a dance of worship? Which ones are about a community gathering? Which ones associate dancing with sexual promiscuity? Which ones demonstrate rebellion from God's way?

Most teens I know are interested in dancing primarily as a social opportunity. Not all dances are sexual, but sometimes a dance that isn't sexual to you might be sexual to someone else. (Also, people who never dance can misuse the sexuality God's given them.)

The truth is that Adventists have always been opposed to dancing that's sexual, especially when it arouses people. (If you're not completely sure of the difference between sexually arousing dancing and dancing that isn't sexual, ask your parents.)

It's good for you and your parents to forge this path with an open channel of communication. Remember, they're on your side, and they want to help you do what's right!

GOING TO THE THEATER

Why do people say we shouldn't go to the theater?
I've read what Ellen White wrote about not going
to the theater or the circus, and Adventists today
seem to have no problem going to the circus.
That seems to be a double standard to me.
And when people tell me that the environment
is bad in a theater, it seems as though they
haven't been to a theater.
Aren't we able to make wise decisions on
what's good and what isn't at a theater? Can you
help me understand what's going on here?

You nailed it—it is a double standard. But it hasn't always been that way. A quick review of Adventist history will prove to be very enlightening.

When the Seventh-day Adventist Church got started more than 100 years ago, the focus was on our unique doctrines, such as the second coming of Christ, the seventh-day Sabbath, death as sleep, the heavenly sanctuary, and a current Spirit of prophecy.

Lifestyle issues, such as not attending the theater, not drinking alcohol, not wearing jewelry, etc., were common beliefs and practices among many different religions in America. Because many Adventists came from these other religions, they simply continued these lifestyle practices, which weren't unique to Adventists at that time.

Ellen White wrote what she did about theaters before motion pictures were even invented. In her day live plays, much like the ones performed on Broadway, were what people went to see in theaters.

More background information reveals that what Ellen White wrote against theaters was based on her experience living in Battle Creek, Michigan. Battle Creek was the railroad stop halfway between Detroit and Chicago—two major cities with major theaters. Big productions that played in these two cities often played in Battle Creek, too. So Battle Creek had everything a big city could boast of theaterwise.

Not surprisingly, the content of most plays included plenty of junk. And the "environment" issue had to do with the type of people attracted to that kind of entertainment and that part of town. Those same elements were often present at the circus, too. That's why Ellen White warned against these attractions. That's hardly surprising.

Ellen White died before the media explosion. So some people figure that a person can watch anything on TV and not be affected by it. Why? Because, after all, Ellen White didn't warn us about TV before she died! (I think that's called "checking your brains at the door"!)

Now that we have easy access to videos, cable TV, satellite dishes, etc., all kinds of viewing options are available. People can easily opt out of ever attending a theater.

But even if you never go to a theater, you still have to make decisions about the bigger issue: entertainment. And movies are simply one form of entertainment.

Looking at the big picture (no pun intended), you'll always need to make wise choices about your entertainment. And the principles you use for making your decisions are the same ones that apply to theaters, videos, the circus, sporting events, skating, and even putt-putt golf!

So when you're facing entertainment choices, keep these guiding principles in mind:

• GARBAGE IN, GARBAGE OUT; QUALITY IN, QUALITY OUT. Check out Philippians 4:8; 2 Peter 1:2-8; and 1 Corinthians 10:31.

• EVERYTHING WE ENCOUNTER SHAPES OUR WORLDVIEW. If we expect people to be trustworthy, not have sex outside of marriage, and not think ethnic jokes are acceptable, why would we want to watch or take part in forms of entertainment that compromise these standards? Check out 2 Corinthians 3:18 and Romans 12:1, 2.

• GOD CAME TO A MESSY ENVIRONMENT—EARTH—ON A MISSION. We're called to enter messy environments just as Jesus did, but we must also be on a mission. It's time to transform our culture instead of being transformed by it. Check out Jesus' prayer for His disciples in John 17:15-18, and pray it for yourself too. It's a good idea to make Jesus your guest everywhere you go.

• TAKE A (GOOD) BREAK. Entertainment can certainly be acceptable. In Mark 6:31 Jesus told His disciples that they needed to take a break. Yet you should be aware that just because you're taking a break, life hasn't stopped. Your mind might be turned off as far as you're concerned, but it's still drinking in everything. According to T. S. Eliot, people are most easily influenced when they're being entertained. So how do you want to be influenced?

As a teenager you're certainly old enough to be making some intelligent decisions about your entertainment. Ideally you'll be able to discuss these principles and choices with your parents, youth leaders, and other adults.

Ask them what they believe and what they practice. Ask them where their gray areas are. Ask them about the double standards they're aware of. Ask them what some of their good choices have been and some choices they made that they later regretted.

Learn from their choices, and ask God to help you make even better ones.

VIDEOS

I want to watch some interesting movies,
but they have some bad language or sex in them.
Would it be OK if I just fast-forward through those parts?
I don't see why people make such a big deal about
those things anyway. It's not as if I've never
heard those words or heard about sex.

Some people avoid movies completely, whether they're in theaters or on video, DVD, laser disc, or TV. Some of their reasons include: they want to avoid evil (or the appearance of evil), they find other activities more fun, or they simply don't have time for it.

But you stated that you want to watch some movies. So how do you decide what to watch or not to watch? If you were a child, I'd choose the movies that you watch. But now you're forming your own guidelines.

Some people simply watch whatever is the newest release. Others choose movies by who stars in them or what category they fit into (comedy, action, sci-fi, etc.). Still others seem to care more about who they're with or where and when they watch a movie.

Recently a friend passed on to me a story of a father who stopped his children from renting a PG-13 movie that had a few questionable elements. When his reasons for not renting the movie met with anger, disappointment, and frustration, he offered to bake his kids some homemade brownies instead.

Later, when he offered them the piping hot brownies, he explained that there was just one catch: the brownies had a cup of dog poop in them. But he assured the kids that there were plenty of other good ingredients in them.

After the kids finished grossing out, Dad had obviously made his point.

Of course, I'm not suggesting that anybody eat brownies with dog poop in them! I'm also not suggesting than anyone should watch a movie that has just a little bit of bad stuff in it.

Here's the ideal: "You'll do best by filling your minds and meditating on things true, noble, reputable, authentic, compelling, gracious—the best, not the worst; the beautiful, not the ugly; things to praise, not things to curse" (Philippians 4:8, Message).

For those who argue that we just need to get used to the world, I'll agree that it's wise for us to know what's going on. But that certainly doesn't mean we need to be a part of it! (See 1 Corinthians 5:9-13.)

Bad language, violence, sex scenes, etc., are actually in the Bible. But the Bible provides God's perspective on these things, which is usually opposite of the way they're presented in movies.

Perhaps the worst part of watching movies is that we become spectators and just drink them in without thinking or responding. Females get presented as bimbos, cheating gets you ahead, might makes right, religious people are stupid, dates should end with bed scenes, alcohol is a part of any good time.

Whenever we view these things without challenging them, they become what we expect. And soon we find that our view of reality has been warped far from God's ideal. And we're the ones least aware of it!

CHRISTIAN ROCK

Is there really any such thing as "Christian rock"?
Would God listen to it or approve of it?

I used to answer this question by saying Christian rock is the devil's attempt to sneak into the church. I would tell people that "Christian rock" is an oxymoron (two opposites put together so they don't make sense, such as "jumbo shrimp"). Consider 2 Corinthians 6:14, 15: "What do righteousness and wickedness have in common? Or what fellowship can light have with darkness? What harmony is there between Christ and Belial? What does a believer have in common with an unbeliever?"

Now I answer questions on "Christian rock" by asking, What is your bias about "Christian rock"? Do you already think it's OK or not OK? I probably won't change your opinion.

If you believe that "Christian rock" is an oxymoron like "Christian pornography," this shows your bias against rock. When I think of "rock" now, I think of Jesus Christ, who is called the Rock (see 1 Corinthians 10:4)—which shows my bias.

If you already think that anything that sounds like rock is automatically from the devil, you won't accept anything I say anyway. If you are still open to considering it, look at Luke 9:49, 50. The disciples of Jesus wanted to stop somebody who was casting out demons, because he was "not one of us." Jesus told them not to stop him, because "whoever is not against you is for you."

Instead of judging "Christian rock" as sounding godly or demonic, judge the fruit it produces (see

Matthew 7:15-20) and test the spirit it creates and shares (see 1 John 4:1-3). Quite frankly, I don't like the sound of some "Christian rock" groups, but when their fruit and the spirit they produce takes people to Jesus, I rejoice even though I detest their sound.

Here are two common sense things to keep in mind when discussing music:

- **MUSICAL PREFERENCES ARE PERSONAL.** This also means that musical tastes/preferences can change.
- **TEEN MUSIC HAS A BAD REPUTATION.** The music young people listen to always seems to get labeled as "terrible" or "worldly" or "satanic" or "You call that music?" or "It's too loud!" by older people. But the critics usually forget that their elders said exactly the same things to them just a decade or two earlier.

I find many criticisms about music laughable—criticisms such as "It makes your pulse rate increase." What's wrong with increasing one's pulse rate? Should we never exercise because it will increase our heart rate?

Two key passages I'd recommend when it comes to listening to music are Philippians 4:8 and Colossians 2:8. The Philippians passage instructs us to keep our minds focused on things that are "true, noble, right, pure, lovely, admirable, excellent, or praiseworthy."

Colossians 2:8 warns us to "see to it that no one takes you captive through hollow and deceptive philosophy, which depends on human tradition and the basic principles of this world rather than on Christ."

Apply these principles to your musical selections as well as to the rest of your decisions. Challenge others to do the same. Does your music increase your faith in God and your love for Him? If so, then keep listening to it. If not, be willing to make good changes or turn it off.

THE PROM

I go to public school, and I've been asked to the prom.
It's on a Saturday night after sundown.
Would it be wrong to go?

It sounds as though you've heard someone say, "You can't go to the prom, because it's on Sabbath [or Friday night]." Well, that's not an issue in your situation. So you get to deal with something closer to the heart of things—the prom itself.

For many students on a high school campus, the prom is the major social event of the year. It's a fun evening with friends and classmates. And when you have a date with someone (especially if your heart skips a beat or two when thinking about them), going to the prom involves extra excitement, hope, and joy (and anxiety)!

But besides skipping the prom because of typical Sabbath conflicts, Adventists often choose to avoid it because of the activities that occur at a prom.

Dancing that stimulates sexual desires can dominate the evening. And will someone sneak vodka into the drink? Is there an expectation from students that—because of the money they invest and the magnitude of the event—the evening should end in sex? If so, Christian standards get compromised.

But that doesn't mean proms are automatically evil. Being with friends, dressing up, developing special friendships, supporting your school, and having fun seem harmless, even wholesome.

Perhaps a good guideline for your question can be found in the last half of Romans 14:23: "Everything that does not come from faith is sin."

Those who desire to be faithful to God ask themselves this question for all their social events, including the prom.

JEWELRY

What's so bad about jewelry?

When the Seventh-day Adventist Church started more than 100 years ago, Christians from a number of denominations didn't wear jewelry, because they felt it drew too much attention to the person wearing it—sort of like a way to show off. Seventh-day Adventists agreed.

Furthermore, because of their strong belief in Jesus' soon return, Seventh-day Adventists spent most of the little money they had on getting the word out about Christ's second coming. That meant no extra cash for jewelry. They considered jewelry a waste of money compared to sharing Jesus (don't you think they were right?).

Now, let's consider another point. Jewelry is easy to see, and some people make quick judgments that a person wearing jewelry is rebelling or sliding away from their faith. It becomes a disturbing sign to others rather than an object of beauty.

Check out what God says about jewelry. I recommend that you read the allegory (parable) in Ezekiel 16.

In that allegory God's people are represented as an abandoned newborn. But God rescues the baby from certain death and nurtures it. Then God says, "I adorned you with jewelry: I put bracelets on your arms and a necklace around your neck, and I put a ring on your nose, earrings on your ears and a beautiful crown on your head" (verses 11, 12).

Evidently God doesn't have a problem with jewelry! But the turning point comes in verse 15: "But you trusted in your beauty and used your fame to become a prostitute."

Jewelry is one element of outward beauty that led the rescued "newborn" to trust in her beauty instead of in God. How tragic that God's people—rescued, nurtured, and blessed by Him—would turn to others and reject Him!

Let me be clear that the story is not about jewelry. Jewelry was simply one of the ways God showed His love for His people. And it was also one of the ways that God's people trusted in themselves rather than in God.

The deeper issue is whether you place emphasis on the shallow exterior or the deeper interior (see 1 Peter 3:3, 4). Outward beauty is so important in the world's eyes, but it is meaningless to God in comparison to a person's inner beauty—their character.

Where are you more beautiful—in outward appearance or in inner character? Where is your emphasis?

Consider this powerful passage from Ellen White concerning the heart of the jewelry matter:

"There are many who try to correct the life of others by attacking what they consider are wrong habits. They go to those whom they think are in error, and point out their defects. They say, 'You don't dress as you should.' They try to pick off the ornaments, or whatever seems offensive, but they do not seek to fasten the mind to the truth. Those who seek to correct others should present the attractions of Jesus. They should talk of His love and compassion, present His example and sacrifice, reveal His Spirit, and they need not touch the subject of dress at all. There is no need to make the dress question the main point of your religion. There is something richer to speak of. Talk of

Christ, and when the heart is converted, everything that is out of harmony with the Word of God will drop off. It is only labor in vain to pick leaves off a living tree. The leaves will reappear. The ax must be laid at the root of the tree, and then the leaves will fall off, never to return" (Ellen White, *Evangelism,* p. 272).

DRINKING

What about the text that says drink in moderation?

Here's the text: "Stop drinking only water, and use a little wine because of your stomach and your frequent illnesses" (1 Timothy 5:23).

What do you think that means? Maybe I should ask, "What do you *want* it to mean?"

Those who want to drink alcohol zero in on this verse, for obvious reasons. But they stay away from a verse like "Wine is a mocker and beer a brawler; whoever is led astray by them is not wise" (Proverbs 20:1).

Let's look into why Paul wrote that advice to Timothy.

Most North Americans are familiar with the advice "Don't drink the water!" when they go to other countries. Young people who go on mission trips sometimes learn this the hard way by getting diarrhea.

We're so accustomed to getting drinking water from the tap, we forget how common it was for people in Bible times to carry some wine with them to purify water for drinking. They would mix two or three times as much water as wine for their drinks. That purified the water and watered down the wine.

Timothy was trying to make it with the water-only routine. But he'd get sick. So Paul told him to drink a little wine to help his stomach.

Is the water you drink safe? If not, you could easily get sick unless you do something to purify the water. That's the reason for this text.

By the way, I've noticed that those who emphasize this text want to drink alcohol, sometimes even feeling that the Bible justifies their desire. It reminds me of how the media have led the general public to think that according to scientific studies, drinking wine makes people healthy (by reducing the likelihood of heart disease).

But researchers such as Dr. Yano write, "Reports of our work in the lay press have, unfortunately, implied that a judicious tipling is a good preventative health measure. This distortion of our conclusions is not justified by the data."

Here's my paraphrase: "If you think drinking alcohol is healthy, get a clue!"

It's usually not wise to base your beliefs on only one text of Scripture. Get a concordance and check out some of the other 200-plus wine verses in the Bible to get a more accurate picture. And get the book *Shall We Dance* (written by . . . me!) and check out the section on alcohol.

EATING MEAT

Why does the church not really want you to eat meat?
The Bible doesn't say meat-eating is a sin.

The bigger issue is health. The church is in favor of good health. You can probably think of a number of areas, besides avoiding meat, that make up the church's health principles: cutting down on sugar and fats; getting enough rest; performing regular exercise; drinking water; eating a balanced diet; not stressing out; getting adequate sunlight; and trusting God.

Why does health matter? According to 1 Corinthians 6:19, 20, our bodies belong to God, and the Holy Spirit lives in us when we give ourselves to Jesus. God has made us as whole people, which includes the physical—our health (see Genesis 2:7).

Because some have made healthful living almost a religion by itself, others have reacted by blatantly disregarding healthy practices, announcing that such actions are "only a matter of health, not salvation." It's true that Jesus will give us a new body when He returns (see 1 Corinthians 15:50-53), but our salvation begins now (see John 5:24), which means our current health matters a great deal. It's more than just health. We are whole people.

As far as "not eating meat" is concerned, meat wasn't even part of humanity's diet until after the Flood (see Genesis 9:3, 4). Seventh-day Adventists continue to follow the specific rules God gave the Israelites about not eating "unclean" meats (see Leviticus 11), such as the animal garbage collectors. Jesus certainly ate meat (see Luke 24:41-43) and even multiplied it for others to eat (see John 6:11).

Don't get tripped up on the meat versus no meat issue. Live as healthfully as you can because your body belongs to God, who saves you and lives in you. Your spiritual life is affected by your physical life since you are a whole person.

INCENSE

People tell me that burning incense is evil.
But how can that be? Didn't they burn incense
in Bible times? I can't seem to get an answer
from anybody. Can you give me one?

I'd be happy to offer you an answer, plus an opportunity to check out for yourself a few passages in the Bible.

When I first read your question, I found it troubling that you couldn't get an answer from anybody. I hope you can find some people willing to study this with you, especially if they can't give you an answer themselves.

I'd recommend that after you study the topic for yourself you share what you find with those who didn't have an answer. Then ask them to study the subject for themselves so you can discuss it. Or study the passages together.

Here are some passages I'd recommend. I looked in a Bible concordance (a reference book or computer program that lists every word used in the Bible and where it's found). The word "incense" appears 121 times in the King James Version. The first mention comes in Exodus, and the last in Revelation. Here are some samples:

• EXODUS 25:6—The Israelites were to donate incense as part of the rest of their offerings.

• EXODUS 30:1, 7, 8—God instructed Moses to build an altar of incense in the Temple. And the Israelites should burn incense on the altar every morning and evening.

• LEVITICUS 10:1—The high priest's sons played around with the incense that was to be holy, and it seriously offended God.

• LEVITICUS **16:12, 13**—Incense was part of the Day of Atonement ceremony, when the high priest went into the Most Holy Place to the mercy seat.

• NUMBERS **16**—In this wild story about people defiant of Moses and Aaron, incense was used by the "bad guys" and the "good guys."

• 1 KINGS **11:8**—Solomon provided altars and incense for his foreign wives to worship their foreign gods.

• PSALM **141:2**—David asked God for his prayer to be like incense.

• ISAIAH **1:13**—Israel's hypocrisy made God sick, so He found their offering of incense detestable.

• LUKE **1:8-13**—Zechariah, the father of John the Baptist, was doing his priestly duty of offering incense at the Temple when an angel told him about the miraculous coming of John the Baptist.

• REVELATION **8:3**—An angel offered incense in the temple in heaven. The incense was mixed with the prayers of the saints.

Check out these passages and others (Jeremiah and Ezekiel have a bunch of them). Incense seems to have been used in religious worship—to God as well as to false gods.

But don't jump to the conclusion that incense was used only in worship. It was like air freshener or perfume. Only when incense that was dedicated for holy use was misused did it become evil.

In more recent times, incense sometimes has been associated with the drug culture as a way to cover the smell of marijuana smoke. But using incense as an air freshener today is no different from lighting scented candles for a nice aroma.

That's my answer, plus some texts to get you started as you study the topic for yourself.

PALM READING

Is it wrong to learn how to read people's palms for fun?

Sounds pretty harmless to me at first glance. I mean, what could be wrong with looking at the lines on a person's hand? Nobody knows what will happen in the future anyway. It's not like you're having a séance or something, right?

Yet here's some counsel that God gave His people just before they entered the Promised Land. I think it provides guidance that will help answer your question. Especially notice the middle part of the passage:

"You will enter the land the Lord your God is giving you. But don't learn to do the terrible things the other nations do. Don't let anyone among you offer his son or daughter as a sacrifice in the fire. Don't let anyone use magic or witchcraft. No one should try to explain the meaning of signs. Don't let anyone try to control others with magic. Don't let them be mediums or try to talk with the spirits of dead people. The Lord hates anyone who does these things. The other nations do these things. That is why the Lord your God will force them out of the land ahead of you. You must be innocent in the presence of the Lord your God" (Deuteronomy 18:9-13, EB).

Some activities have a combination of good and bad results. But others seem to be directly associated with Satan and the demonic world—things such as witchcraft, séances, Ouija boards, tarot cards, palm reading, horoscopes, channeling, and getting "energy" from crystals.

Not everyone who dabbles in these activities gets caught up in them or automatically becomes part of the devil's force—but I'd definitely stay away from them if I were you! You don't want to open the door to Satan in any way. And you only have to see one or two people who got messed up with it, and you'll want to steer clear of it forever.

Here's an alternative. If you're innocently looking for a little bit of fun and adventure, ask God to use you to make a difference in somebody else's life, regardless of the palm lines they have (or don't have). You'll definitely need input from the Supernatural—and some motivation! But why not get in tune with the winning team instead of the losing one?

HYPNOTISM

I'd like to know what's wrong with hypnotism.
I was looking at a TV program this week, and
this guy was hypnotizing eight people. They were
doing funny stuff. It was kind of cool to see people
doing stuff they don't remember doing at all.

Probably the major negative issue has to do with handing yourself over to the control and manipulation of someone else. I suppose it's up to the hypnotist to decide what you will do without you remembering. Could be good, could be bad.

What difference does it make if you don't remember it anyway?

Well, let's try this out with some everyday situations. Under hypnosis while at school, you talk only to people who are wearing red. Imagine the surprise and perplexity of friends you ignore because they're not wearing red. Or how about those strangers or people you don't usually talk to? But they're wearing red today, so you engage in conversation with them.

Hey, wait. It gets better. Tomorrow you're not hypnotized. So you go to school as if nothing unusual happened yesterday. Isn't this great? Now you get to try to undo the fact that you ignored your friends (even though you don't remember it). And now you have to deal with those people who thought you had become friendly, when you really didn't mean it.

But that's just the casual stuff. Most relationships have ups and downs, give and take, sharing. Who would willingly hand themselves over to someone else, especially a stranger, to control them? What kind of relationship is that?

God created us free to choose. Satan's kingdom can be characterized as one without choice. Satan seeks to control. For a negative but graphic illustration of that, check out Mark 5:2-5—the story of the demoniac.

We're born with a sinful human nature, which has us in the grip of its control. According to John 8:34, "Anyone who sins is enslaved" (Clear Word). The contrast comes two verses later: "If the Son [Jesus] sets you free, you will be free indeed" (verse 36).

To be controlled by someone else is Satan's way. Being free is God's way. This means if your religion is "controlling," perhaps you need Jesus to set you free!

When I rely completely on God, "there is now a new nature working in me giving me a totally different motive for serving God. This new nature is a gift from the Holy Spirit who through Christ has freed me from the controlling power of my sinful nature which always stands ready to put me back on the road to death" (Romans 8:2, Clear Word).

"Funny" may not be the best measure to judge something. Being free counts for a lot more.

PEOPLE PROBLEMS

WHAT ABOUT HYPOCRITES?

Everyone preaches acceptance, but are judgmental pastors hypocrites? What do we do about them?

Yes, judgmental pastors are hypocrites. But then, who isn't a hypocrite?

Just when you might be tempted to think you have it all together, God can reveal something that's been oblivious to you (even though others might have noticed it for years!). We all have blind spots (in addition to the things we still struggle with while wanting to live completely for Jesus).

Then we have the challenge to go beyond the basic messages of Scripture and find the heart and soul of their meaning. Jesus tried doing this with the Pharisees, terrific examples of hypocrites (see Matthew 23:13-28).

And when teaching the multitudes on the mountainside, Jesus attempted to expand their understanding of living for Him. Many thought that as long as they hadn't murdered somebody, they had obeyed the law that says "Thou shalt not kill." But Jesus pointed out that getting angry with someone is a form of murdering them (Matthew 5:21, 22).

When your understanding begins broadening like this, it becomes obvious that most of us are hypocrites!

I've heard some people say that they don't attend church, because there are so many hypocrites there. But I can't think of a better place for a hypocrite than church! Hypocrites need help. And the church is a hospital for people who want to worship God and get their lives back together so they can live for Him.

One other thing. Don't misuse Matthew 7:1: "Do not judge, or you too will be judged." In that same section Jesus told the people not to give dogs what is sacred and advised them not to throw their pearls to the pigs (verse 6). Sounds as though it takes some judgment to determine whether you're dealing with a dog, a pig, or something else.

This passage—Matthew 7:1-6—isn't a message saying "Don't use your judgment." Verse 4 simply points out how ridiculous it is to offer to help a person get a speck out of their eye when there's an entire log in your own. That's totally hypocritical!

Verse 5 suggests that we first take the log out of our own eye, and then we will see clearly to remove the speck out of someone else's eye.

So what should you do about your hypocritical pastor? Get the log out of your own eye so you can see clearly to remove the speck from your pastor's eye.

If you don't have a clue what log is in your eye, try asking the pastor (or someone who knows you well). We can really help each other.

I'VE BEEN WRONGED

*What do you do when someone has wronged you,
but they make no effort to ask forgiveness,
or they think that they were right?*

This is a biggy, and it seems to happen all the time. It's what ruins friendships.

With every friendship you will have times when you mess up—or at least it looks like you messed up. The same is true for your friend. If you are friends with someone long enough, eventually the other person will do something wrong—something that puts you down, makes you look like a fool, or just ticks you off.

Here are two recommendations, both from the book of Matthew. One has to do with justice—doing what's right. The other emphasizes mercy—doing what's kind.

The first recommendation focuses on getting things straightened out (see Matthew 18:15-17). When people feel they've been wronged, most go talk to others about it. This earns them sympathy and makes them more sure they were right.

But Jesus said to start with the person you believe has wronged you, and talk it out together. If that doesn't work, take another open-minded person with you. If that still doesn't work, bring more people.

The second recommendation (the "merciful" one, found in Matthew 5:21-24) might be even more difficult than the first, and you can't do it without God.

Jesus said that if you're worshiping God and remember that somebody has "something against you," you need to stop worshiping temporarily, go immediately to that person, take the initiative, and make things right. That's right, you take the initiative, even if it's the other person's fault!

See what I mean about needing God on this? Then you'll be able to worship Him again.

By the way, if you want to hold out for justice and forget the mercy bit, check out the story Jesus gave in Matthew 18:23-35. Don't treat the other person the way they deserve. Treat them the way God treats you!

MY PARENTS GIVE GUILT TRIPS

*Why is it if I do something wrong, my parents
have to bring up the Bible, what God wants
me to do, and how God wants me to be?*

It sounds as though when you do something wrong, you don't want anybody to correct you. Or perhaps you just get weary of feeling beat over the head, especially when you already feel guilty.

It's quite common for teens to feel a desire for freedom, especially freedom from those who try to impose rules on them. Sometimes you just want "to chill" instead of always getting corrected.

But I'm a parent now, and I feel a great sense of responsibility for my child. In fact, much more than she feels for herself!

I *really* feel responsibility when I read passages such as Deuteronomy 6:6, 7: "These commandments that I give you today are to be upon your hearts. Impress them on your children. Talk about them when you sit at home and when you walk along the road, when you lie down and when you get up."

This text is where many parents get the idea of family worship, plus being aware of all the teachable moments.

I've been surprised at how much I end up correcting my daughter. And as I think about it, I can imagine my daughter asking the same question you did!

Now that we've looked at why your parents react the way they do, let's see why you feel the way you do. It's natural that when we do something wrong, we feel guilty. And we certainly don't want people to point out our mistakes.

This is what makes sin so vicious. It makes us guilty, and then when we feel guilty, we avoid being corrected (which just *keeps* us feeling guilty).

When we do something wrong, we *need* to be corrected. Some parents might add an extra burst of authority by claiming that God feels the same way they do about your disobedience.

Actually, the *purpose* of God's law is to point out that we're guilty. Paul explains that the law, though good, can't save us—it can only show us that we *need* to be saved.

In other words, the law shows us that we need Jesus to save us. "The Scriptures have declared that we are all prisoners of sin, so the only way to receive God's promise is to believe in Jesus Christ. . . . The law was our guardian and teacher to lead us until Christ came. So now, through faith in Christ, we are made right with God" (Galatians 3:22-24, NLT).

So instead of getting defensive when you've done something wrong, go to Jesus to receive forgiveness and cleansing.

DEALING WITH PICKY PEOPLE

Why do people pick on other people?

I heard this truism from Chris Miller when he was the chaplain at Blue Mountain Academy: "Hurt people hurt people."

It really makes sense. The people who hurt others usually do so because of the hurt they've already received. That's one of the added curses of sin—it repeats itself.

Here's an analogy from lifeguard training. One of the ironies of helping a drowning person is that the person will often try to drown the individual who came to save them. Without even realizing it, the drowning person grabs onto the lifesaver and pulls him or her down. A drowning person can actually drown himself or herself and the lifesaver.

I'll let you make the connections between lifesaving and picking on others.

Often those who pick on others do so out of their own insecurity. They might not even be aware of what they're doing! So while those who are picked on deserve sympathy and support, those who pick on others are the ones who really need help and a sense of acceptance that only God can give them.

Then there's the tendency to pick on those who are different from us. Physical differences are initially most obvious. But remember, "Man looks at the outward appearance, but the Lord looks at the heart" (1 Samuel 16:7).

How do you relate to others, especially those who are different from you? Two helpful texts in this regard are these familiar ones: "For God so loved the world that he gave his one and only Son, that whoever believes in him shall not perish but have eternal life" (John 3:16), and "There is neither Jew nor Greek, slave nor free, male nor female, for you are all one in Christ Jesus" (Galatians 3:28).

When you look at others through God's eyes, you simply can't pick on them. Why not go with Paul's counsel: "Encourage one another and build each other up, just as in fact you are doing" (1 Thessalonians 5:11).

MY FRIEND'S NOT ACTING LIKE A CHRISTIAN

How do I relate to a friend who says he's a Christian and yet lives a lifestyle that the Bible clearly says is wrong? What can I say to him, and how can I say it in a way that won't cause him to leave the church and God?

Your friend probably matches one of the following descriptions:

1. BLIND SPOT: "I don't even see that my lifestyle is clearly wrong."

2. I KNOW, AND I FEEL GUILTY: "I see that my lifestyle is wrong, and I'm embarrassed about it."

3. I KNOW, AND I DON'T FEEL GUILTY: "I know what my lifestyle is, and I don't think it's wrong." Or "I know what my lifestyle is, and I used to think it was wrong. But it no longer bothers my conscience."

For someone in the first category, I'd recommend sharing your perspective as a friend. That means giving that person "I" messages instead of "you" messages.

An "I" message might be "I'm concerned that the joy of Sabbath won't be part of your life because of your Sabbath job." A "you" message would be "You're breaking the Sabbath, and that's wrong."

A friend in the second category needs support and encouragement more than pointing out the problem. Remember, you can support your friend without agreeing with the wrong element of his lifestyle. And if you think additional support or guidance from another person would help, make that a reality if your friend is open to it.

If your friend fits the third category, you'll probably feel challenged to continue supporting him, since you disagree with his lifestyle. In this situation it's probably more important to listen to your friend's perspective than to give yours. Your friend isn't likely to listen to you until he feels you've listened to him.

In John 16:12, 13 Jesus told His disciples, "I have much more to say to you, more than you can now bear. But when he, the Spirit of truth, comes, he will guide you into all truth."

Jesus said that after spending three years training His disciples! So if your friend isn't open to change now, be assured that the Spirit will still prod him in the future.

When it comes to relating to a friend who's clearly living a lifestyle apart from God, first of all accept *him,* not his lifestyle. And if that seems ridiculous, remember that God accepts us where we are.

Second, support your friend as a *friend,* even if you don't agree with his lifestyle.

And finally, encourage openness for growth—both in your friend and in yourself. Be willing for your friend to help you in your lifestyle issues that aren't Christlike (yes, you have them). The Spirit isn't finished with you yet either.

BAD ADVICE?

My friends always come to me for advice.
What if I give them bad advice?

Everybody needs advice (or counseling) at various times. But most people don't go to official counselors. The person they're most likely to go to is a friend who's a good listener. It sounds like you're a good listener!

Hurting people don't turn to wise or witty people as much as they turn to someone they trust—usually a friend. In fact, most trained counselors will first establish a relationship with people they're counseling in order to gain their trust.

Some schools and churches set up "peer counseling" programs for junior high or senior high students. "Can peers be good counselors?" people ask. They can if the teen counselors learn skills that make them better listeners. When individuals become good listeners, others automatically come to them for unofficial counseling.

When I use good listening skills on a regular basis, people come to me for advice. When I cut people off, speak about my interests instead of theirs, or get distracted easily when they're talking to me, guess what? They quit coming!

The last part of Proverbs 18:24 reads "There is a friend who sticks closer than a brother." It's comforting to know that God wants to be our closest friend, even more intimate and trustworthy than a loyal brother. You can trust God, and you can go to Him for advice.

You also asked, "What if I give bad advice?" That will happen. Or maybe your advice is good, but not necessarily for that person or for that time. I'm not suggesting you shouldn't give advice, though. I'm just warning you that not everything you say will be perfect.

The Bible speaks of Jesus being a "Wonderful Counselor" who is also a "Mighty God, Everlasting Father, Prince of Peace" (Isaiah 9:6). When Jesus left His disciples to return to heaven, He promised that "the Counselor, the Holy Spirit, whom the Father will send in my name, will teach you all things and will remind you of everything I have said to you" (John 14:26).

Tough situations drive people to prayer. And it's appropriate for you to pray with your friend for guidance, with an openness to follow God's leading. Tough situations also provide additional motivation for Bible study—to discover God's counsel in similar types of situations.

Recently I was counseling somebody in between speaking sessions at a camp meeting. In spite of using good listening skills and giving the best advice I could come up with, I knew I wasn't getting through. The young person finally blurted out, "It's OK, Pastor Steve. I know you're really trying, but what you're saying just doesn't work."

I appreciated the honesty, yet I felt disappointed that I didn't have the perfect recipe for the troubled teen.

Here's my final advice: Be a good listener. And when you give your perspective on things, make it clear that this is simply your perspective. What people do with your advice is their business and their responsibility, not yours. And that needs to be clear to both of you!

WHAT'S INSIDE COUNTS

Why do people seem to care more about what's
on the outside of a person than on the inside?

Because it's easier to see what's outside, that's why! Let's face it, we're curious creatures. So as we observe or discover "surface" things about people, we're tempted to make judgments about what's inside them.

On the other hand, some people may have given up even trying to discover what's inside people. That leaves them to place all their emphasis on externals—their own and those around them. Can you think of people who seem to spend most of their waking hours fine-tuning their outside, while their inside either rots or lies dormant?

The opposite of these people are those who care only about the inside—they couldn't care less about what's on the outside. Sloppy professors come to mind.

Then there are many people who are concerned about what's inside other people—but they look at the outside for evidence of what's inside. For example, they might ask such questions as "If you really care about me [inside], then why do you say so many things that put me down in front of others [outside]?" Or "If you really don't care about me [inside], why do you always hang around me [outside]?" They try to discover what's inside by outward signs.

When I was a teen, spiritual people didn't wear blue jeans (only hippies did that). And satanic dope smokers played guitars. Now that everybody wears jeans and guitars are acceptable instruments to play in church, teens are judged by different standards. But the truth is, when teens do trendy things (outside), it tends to threaten the way people judge their insides.

I think the best candidate for the most-misunderstood-person-of-all-time would be Jesus. He didn't fit what people were looking for on the outside. And then they didn't catch on to what He was about inside, either.

One time the religious leaders wanted to kill Jesus because He healed a man on Sabbath (usually a good outward action, but doing it on Sabbath made it "bad"). The miracle itself was good (outside), but it made the jealous priests angry (inside).

Nobody seemed to catch on to the "inside" information Jesus was offering by His action—that Sabbath is a day for doing good, not a day to be paranoid about possibly doing something wrong!

In this context Jesus said, "Stop judging by mere appearances, and make a right judgment" (John 7:24). That's relevant counsel for us.

SUICIDE AND SALVATION

Are there instances in which people commit suicide, but will still go to heaven? What if the person couldn't think straight because they were so messed up? Are they still held accountable?

Will someone who committed suicide be in heaven? Most people would initially say "No" or "I doubt it." They figure that the person's last act before death was killing someone (themselves). Something so horrible (or possibly selfish) would keep that person out of heaven, wouldn't it?

That takes us back to thinking that our actions (behavior) will keep us out of heaven—which leads us to believe that our actions (behavior) are what get us into heaven too. Whoops! Let's not get caught up in that again. If everyone who goes to heaven gets there as a gift from Jesus, then suicide isn't a good way to tell whether or not a person will be in heaven.

Let's consider a few examples of suicide in the Bible. One example is Judas (see Matthew 27:3-5). After turning traitor to Jesus (and realizing that Jesus wasn't going to free Himself), Judas couldn't deal with what he had done, so he committed suicide.

In the Old Testament, Ahithophel committed suicide when Absalom didn't follow his advice to pursue and wipe out King David immediately (see 2 Samuel 17:23).

And what about Samson? He committed suicide and multiple murders as his last act (see Judges 16:30).

Most of us would feel quite certain that Samson won't be in heaven because of his questionable lifestyle and his final act of suicide. But when we read about the people of faith in Hebrews 11, Samson gets mentioned as an example of great faith (see Hebrews 11:32, 39, 40), someone who will receive his eternal reward with the rest of the faithful when Jesus returns. Go figure!

Deep and continuous depression can make individuals more susceptible to suicide. People consider suicide when their other options seem worse than death.

Peter was probably at the verge of suicide after he denied Christ and went back to Gethsemane and wept bitterly. As strange as it may seem, when people are ready to give up on life, they might be ready to give Jesus a try.

I suppose when we attend a funeral, we'll always feel more at ease about the deceased person's eternal destiny if they were a faithful church member who died of old age rather than someone who committed suicide.

HOW DO I SAVE MY FAMILY?

I was wondering, how do I save my family?

You don't save your family; *Christ* does. And you can't make your family choose to be saved. According to Deuteronomy 24:16, children and parents are responsible for their own decisions relating to whether or not they are saved. In other words, your family members have to choose for themselves, just as you do.

But that probably misses the crux of your question. I doubt if you're looking for someone to blame if your family isn't saved. More than likely the real issue is that you really want your family to be saved, so you want to do whatever it takes for that to happen.

Deuteronomy 4:9 and Deuteronomy 6:5-9 command parents to teach their children about God. But even teaching children about God doesn't guarantee they will choose God for themselves. The Old Testament ends with a promise that God will turn the hearts of the parents to their children and vice versa (see Malachi 4:6). Your concern for your family reminds me of this promise.

I also think of the image of the new earth, where "the wolf will live with the lamb, the leopard will lie down with the goat . . . and a little child will lead them" (Isaiah 11:6). I smile as I realize that many who will be in heaven will be there because they followed a young person to Jesus.

What can you do to save your family?
• Pray for them to choose Jesus for themselves.
• Choose Jesus for yourself and live for Him.
• Talk to your family members (honestly, sincerely,

kindly) about your concern for their salvation.
- Invite them to accept Jesus (as their Saviour).
- Listen to their response(s).
- Honor their choice.
- Never give up.

LIVING FOR HIM

I'M SCARED TO WITNESS

I want to tell people about God, but I'm nervous.
How can I witness in a calm way?

Most of us (including youth and adults) believe we should tell others about God, but that doesn't mean we do it. We're afraid—afraid of blowing it, doing it wrong, being rejected, laughed at, or dissed.

Then guilt piles up when we read Jesus' words in Matthew 10:32, 33: "Whoever acknowledges me before men, I will also acknowledge him before my Father in heaven. But whoever disowns me before men, I will disown him before my Father in heaven."

After reading those verses, we figure that Jesus will have to disown us before God. But if it's any consolation, consider Peter's promise to stand for Jesus to the death (Matthew 26:34, 35). Then Peter ended up denying that he even knew Jesus (verses 69-75). So much for telling people about God!

I've found that telling people about God requires some R and R. The first R stands for being *real*. We must share who Jesus is to us and what He means to us. The first few times I tried doing this, I discovered that I had to know Jesus for myself instead of relying on what everybody else says about Him.

The second R stands for *relationship*. We must get to know people before we talk about Jesus with them. That way we can reach them with what they need to hear.

For instance, if we discover that someone is stressed out, we can point out that Jesus is the one who chills (Matthew 11:28-30; Psalm 23). When somebody is bored and looking for excitement, we can present Jesus as the God and Man of action (John 2 gives a couple examples, or check out Mark 12 for a showdown).

By developing a relationship with people, we "earn the right" to be heard when it comes to sharing our God with them.

But the vital requirement for witnessing is having God (through the Holy Spirit) in us. When Peter had the Holy Spirit dwelling in him (Acts 2), he spoke boldly to large groups of people, to leaders, and to individuals. Sometimes his message was popular, and sometimes it wasn't.

According to the book *Steps to Christ*, when we accept Jesus as the one who saves us by forgiving our sins, we want to share Him with others. But if we don't share the good news about Him, we'll lose the desire we initially had.

So my final advice is this: Ask the Holy Spirit into your life. When the Holy Spirit moves inside you, you'll speak and not worry about the results. And remember: be real and build relationships with people. Then go for it, and watch incredible things happen!

What Can I Say?

*How can I share what Seventh-day Adventists
believe without offending people?*

Here are two guidelines (both from 1 Peter) on how
to share the Gospel with others:

**1. Some people will be offended no matter what you
say.** First Peter 2:7, 8 says this: "Yes, he [Christ] is very
precious to you who believe; and to those who reject
him, well—'The same Stone that was rejected by the
builders has become the Cornerstone, the most honored and important part of the building.' And the
Scriptures also say, 'He is the Stone that some will
stumble over, and the Rock that will make them fall.'
They will stumble because they will not listen to God's
Word, nor obey it, and so this punishment must follow—that they will fall" (TLB).

2. There's no need to go around offending others.
First Peter 3:15 tells us, "Quietly trust yourself to Christ
your Lord and if anybody asks why you believe as you
do, be ready to tell him, and do it in a gentle and respectful way" (TLB).

Sometimes people pick out strange or minor things
as the way to describe Seventh-day Adventists—
"They're vegetarians"; "They don't dance"; "They go to
church on the 'wrong' day"; "They do a lot of medical
work"; "They have their own schools"; etc.

Adventists sometimes are confused with other
groups—"Don't you have a special choir in Salt Lake
City?" "Do you have to go out in groups of two and
argue with people on their doorsteps?" "Are you the
ones who won't accept blood transfusions?" "Don't you

people go around on bicycles wearing dark pants and white dress shirts?"

When people ask me what Seventh-day Adventists believe, I usually start with the fact that we're Christians. I tell them that we depend completely on Jesus to forgive us and save us. And we accept salvation as a gift from Him.

Most Christians quickly identify with this, but then they want to know what makes Adventists distinctive from other Christians.

Sometimes I stay with the basic areas of Christian agreement, such as the promise of heaven, the gift of the Holy Spirit in our lives, developing a relationship with Jesus, living for God by serving others, believing that the Bible is God's inspired message to us, etc.

Other times I go into what makes us unique. I start by describing the elements of our name: Seventh-day Adventist. The word "Adventist" gives a clear indication that we emphasize the "Advent," or return of Jesus to take us home with Him. We live our lives with this hope clearly in mind. Most other Christians consider themselves Adventist in this sense too!

The first part of our name, "Seventh-day," highlights the fact that we worship on the day God set aside at the Creation of this world. In fact, throughout Bible times God's people have worshiped on the seventh day. It wasn't until after Bible times that people began to worship on the first day of the week instead of on the seventh day.

We believe that if God had wanted to make that change, it would have been made in the Bible, not after the Bible was complete. And just as the Bible says that God rested on the seventh day of Creation (Genesis 2:1-3), the Sabbath symbolizes the rest we experience by trusting Jesus to save us instead of trying to work our way to heaven (Hebrews 4:9, 10).

Other doctrines of special significance to Seventh-day Adventists include:

- **VIEWING DEATH AS SLEEP UNTIL JESUS RETURNS.** We don't believe that ghosts are floating around or that anyone is burning in hell right now.
- **AN ACTIVE HOLY SPIRIT.** We believe that the Holy Spirit provides spiritual gifts to God's people so they can serve others the same way Jesus did.
- **A UNIQUE BLEND OF FORGIVENESS AND JUSTICE. AT THE** judgment day God's loving justice will finally make sense to everyone. (For more on what Seventh-day Adventists believe, check out *A Reason to Believe, It's My Choice,* or *Seventh-day Adventists Believe* . . . all published by the Review and Herald Publishing Association, 1-800-765-6955).

When people discuss what they believe and why they believe it, there's bound to be disagreement. So it's usually better to share what has made Jesus real to *you* and why *you* are a Seventh-day Adventist. Make it personal, not just a list of items to prove a point.

Practice sharing with others in your church before you try it out on those who aren't Seventh-day Adventists. And don't forget the first two principles at the beginning of this column!

MY PRAYERS AREN'T ANSWERED

*Every time I've prayed for someone, that person
has died. Now I'm scared to death myself.
I don't want people to die because I'm praying
for them. What should I do?*

My guess is that you've prayed for God to heal somebody who was sick, perhaps a grandparent or someone dying of cancer or injured in a terrible accident. And then that person or persons died after you prayed for their healing.

That brings up the issue of what prayer is all about. Some people emphasize that the purpose of prayer is to communicate with God so the two of you can be friends. It's not so much about asking for favors ("Please make Grandpa well," "Please help me find the car keys," etc.) as it is about talking and listening—interacting with God, your Creator and friend.

Yet while prayer is indeed a channel for communicating with God, Jesus Himself urged His followers to ask God for things (Matthew 7:7-11). In fact, Jesus pointed out that if earthly parents willingly respond to the requests of their children, how much more will our heavenly Father respond to us! (See also Romans 8:31, 32.)

God wants us to ask Him for things, and there's no better place to go when we or those around us have a need than to Him.

Sometimes when I read the Bible, though, it sounds as if absolutely everything we pray for will be given to us. But I know from experience that God doesn't grant my every wish.

And I don't really want Him to. Actually, I just want God to do what's best for me and for the people I pray for.

Now, when it comes to death, I'm certain that God is against it. He's the author of life (John 10:10; 1 John 5:11-13). But like you, I've prayed for people to recover, and then they've died.

Yet every person born on earth is subject to death—at least until Jesus comes. In fact, death will be the last enemy God will destroy (1 Corinthians 15:26).

On the other hand, many people have recovered when prayers were offered for them. But eventually they too will die.

That's why heaven will be a great reunion time. There'll be no more separation by death, and we'll be able to enjoy face-to-face communication with God.

Until then, pray more. There's much that God wants to do for you and for others through you. And it's great to talk with our Creator and Saviour and to come to know Him as a friend.

MY PRAYERS *ARE* ANSWERED!

*I don't know what to pray for anymore! It seems
like everything I sincerely ask for happens,
then later I regret my requests. I know I can't go
through life without praying just so I can avoid this.
Do you have any suggestions?*

It seems more common for people to feel as if their prayers aren't answered than to worry that everything they sincerely ask for will happen. While some people may tell you "You have it made!" when it comes to praying, I'm sure at times you feel as though you have quite a burden to carry.

Your situation reminds me of James 5:16: "The prayer of a righteous [person] is powerful and effective."

Remember Elijah? He was a human like us. He prayed earnestly to God that it wouldn't rain, and it didn't rain for three and a half years. Then when he prayed for rain, the heavens sent rain and the earth produced crops.

Oh, to have the faith and powerful prayers of Elijah! Maybe you're one of the few who does!

Maybe you've been given an extra gift of faith and intercessory prayer. That doesn't make you better than anyone else; it simply equips you to minister to and for others in ways many can't or don't.

You're correct in anticipating that if you stop praying, you'll regret it later. Keep it up! Your life won't necessarily be easy, but it will be supernaturally exciting! And you will become more and more Christlike because of what you will go through.

Things that typically hinder the effectiveness of our prayers include falling into sin, failure to forgive others, not asking forgiveness from others and God, thinking we're a hotshot, and not submitting to others.

Two parting thoughts:

• DON'T GET SIDETRACKED BY HOLDING BACK OR QUESTIONING YOURSELF IF OTHERS THINK YOU'RE TOO YOUNG TO HAVE A POTENT PRAYER LIFE. You're not! First Timothy 4:12 says, "Don't let anyone look down on you because you are young, but set an example for the believers in speech, in life, in love, in faith and in purity."

• DON'T EXPECT OTHERS TO HAVE YOUR SAME GIFT OF PRAYER. The Spirit gives different gifts to each person to benefit the body of Christ—His church. You're a vital piece of the puzzle, but you're not the whole picture. Check out the words of wisdom in Ephesians 4:7, 11-13.

I DON'T UNDERSTAND THE BIBLE

After I read part of the Bible, it seems like
I can't always remember what I've read. And
sometimes I don't understand everything I read. I've
prayed to have deeper understanding. What should I do?

Don't read the Bible as if you have to do a book report or write some kind of summary of it. The purpose of reading the Bible is to be in contact with God.

It's actually possible to read the Bible and miss

what it's all about. That's what happened with the religious leaders in Jesus' day. Jesus told them, "You search the Scriptures because you believe they give you eternal life. But the Scriptures point to me! Yet you refuse to come to me so that I can give you this eternal life" (John 5:39, 40, NLT).

It's more important to keep going back to the Bible than just to memorize portions of it. Yet I recommend memorizing Scripture. Psalm 119:11 says: "I have hidden your word in my heart that I might not sin against you."

You can write out a verse on a 3 x 5 card and practice it until you have it memorized. Then add another card with another verse that you've found meaningful. As you memorize more, it gets easier. And as you use the verses, they'll stay fresh in your thinking.

Another good practice is to underline and make marks in your own Bible. There are times when I'll just skim over portions of my Bible, reading the parts that are underlined because they stood out to me before.

I also add lots of notes and cross-references, sometimes during sermons and sometimes during my own personal devotions. The more marked-up my Bible is, the more useful it is to me.

As far as increasing your understanding of the Bible is concerned, you've started in the right place—with prayer! Here are some additional tips after you pray:

• CHECK OUT THE VERSES BEFORE AND AFTER YOUR PASSAGE to get more background about what you're studying (the literary context). Sometimes you'll need to look in a Bible commentary to find out what was happening when that book was written (the historical context). You can also read what a Bible commentary says about the particular passage you're studying.

• START A SMALL STUDY GROUP. Sometimes just having somebody else's input will give you new insights. And by discussing things, you'll find that your own understanding will take shape better than it would have by studying on your own.

• **DIRECT YOUR QUESTIONS TO A RESPECTED STUDENT OF THE BIBLE,** such as a pastor, parent, teacher, another teen with spiritual insight, or *Insight* magazine.

• **MAKE UNDERSTANDING A MATTER OF MORE PRAYER.** Pray through the passage, and listen for God's impressions. Keep praying about it.

Then recognize that you might be trying to remember everything you've heard and read about the Bible when what you really need to do is keep returning there to make contact with Jesus. Keep coming back to Scripture in search of your Saviour.

WHAT'S ONE KEY TEXT?

What is one Bible text against drugs, drinking, and premarital sex?

If you want one text against drugs, drinking, and premarital sex, I'd suggest 1 Corinthians 6:19-20. (I know that's two verses, but it's a complete thought.) Here's what it says:

"Haven't you yet learned that your body is the home of the Holy Spirit God gave you, and that he lives within you? Your own body does not belong to you. For God has bought you with a great price. So use every part of your body to give glory back to God, because he owns it" (TLB).

The context in this verse is sexuality. But the principle of belonging to God applies to drugs, drinking, overeating, inadequate sleep, lack of exercise, and any other abuse you can think of.

First Thessalonians 4:3-8 (Phillips) is pretty catchy

too. The last sentence reads, "It is not for nothing that the Spirit God gives us is called the *Holy* Spirit."

If you want one Bible text *for* positive choices, I'd recommend John 10:10. *The Living Bible* presents the words of Jesus this way: "The thief's purpose is to steal, kill and destroy. My purpose is to give life in all its fullness." You might have heard it this way: "I am come that they might have life, and that they might have it more abundantly" (King James Version).

If you're not a Christian, you can learn from the trial-and-error method, or learn from what's happened to others. It's called choices and consequences. That's a biblical principle too. Check it out in Galatians 6:7, 8.

But you can save yourself a lot of pain and permanent damage by living by God's principle of "Life in all its fullness." Those who want big payoffs know that giving in to the temptation of the moment usually retards their progress toward their bigger goal. God is guiding you to bigger goals. Go for abundant living!

WHY DON'T I CHANGE?

What can you do when you are already doing everything you think God wants you to (because you love Him and want to serve Him), but you don't see any change in your life?

What changes are you expecting? Doing everything you think God wants you to from a motivation of love and service hits the core of what's important.

But let's look at the story of David; his example shows that God's blessing doesn't always come with obvious changes. According to 1 Samuel 16:13, when Samuel anointed David to become the next king, "from that day on the Spirit of the Lord came upon David in power."

Wouldn't you expect David to be crowned king right after that? But no, he went back to tending sheep. Then he played his harp for a depressed king, killed Goliath, and spent several years hiding in the wilderness from Saul.

Even after Saul's death, David became king of only the tribe of Judah. And it wasn't until seven years later that the other 11 tribes asked him to become their king too.

I wonder if David, like you, was looking for more change in his life and wondering why it took so long.

And we often think of the apostle Paul preaching to crowds, starting churches, and creating riots. Much of the book of Acts records his actions.

But after his conversion, Paul actually spent perhaps as long as three years in the desert of Arabia getting his theology corrected by God. I wonder if he was expecting more active changes during those private tutoring sessions.

Even Jesus didn't begin the ministry we're familiar with until He was 30 years old.

So what changes can you expect? Romans 8:29 promises you a likeness of Jesus, which includes the spiritual gifts of "love, joy, peace, patience, kindness, goodness, faithfulness, gentleness and self-control" (Galatians 5:22, 23).

As a teenager I remember reading 1 Peter 2:20, 21: "If you suffer for doing good and you endure it, this is commendable before God. To this you were called, because Christ suffered for you, leaving you an example, that you should follow in his steps."

At that time I couldn't think of any real suffering I had endured for Christ. It made me wonder if I really was a Christian. My mom assured me that I was and that I would certainly experience suffering in due time.

I can testify that I've been very blessed. But even so, I've had some suffering in my life, and it's been enough. Perhaps that's why James wrote, "Consider it pure joy, my brothers, whenever you face trials of many kinds, because you know that the testing of your faith develops perseverance" (James 1:2, 3).

Enjoy the calm while it lasts, be ready for the storms that hit you, and keep your focus on loving and serving God. It may not happen immediately, but believe me, your life will change!

USE IT OR LOSE IT

In Sabbath school we were talking about how
God wants us to use our talents. Is it true
that if we don't use them we won't go to heaven?

Wow, what a guilt trip!

In the parable of the talents in Matthew 25:14-30, it's true that the person who didn't use his one talent got berated by his master, stripped of the talent, and cast into the darkness "where there will be weeping and gnashing of teeth" (Matthew 25:30).

Jesus used parables to share unique insights into aspects of God and His kingdom. Parables can open new understandings, but they can also cloud a person's comprehension (see Matthew 13:13-15), especially when we try to carry the parable's meaning too far.

When we get too literal with parables, we find that things don't always make sense. Sometimes a parable might even seem to contradict other established truths clearly outlined in the Bible.

For example, in the parable of the 10 virgins

(Matthew 25:1-13), we learn the need to have adequate oil to last through the night. Some people find extra meaning in the fact that even the wise virgins slept while waiting.

But to get too literal—to make it seem that only females (and only virgins, excluding married people) are allowed into heaven—obviously goes beyond the meaning of the parable.

If you like parables and could use some help interpreting them, check out *Christ's Object Lessons,* by Ellen White. You'll find the parable of the talents discussed on pages 353-360.

In the parable of the talents the focus is indeed on utilizing what God has given you. But some people, including some youth, cop out of making a difference because they think what they have to offer doesn't seem as significant as what others have to give.

Nonsense! God actually takes the responsibility for increasing our talents. Our part is to commit what we have to Him, not bury what He's given by doing nothing.

The parable of the talents isn't about how to get to heaven. Better parables on that subject would be the story of the wedding feast and wedding garment (Matthew 22:1-14) or even the parable of the workers in the vineyard (Matthew 20:1-16).

Don't buy the lie that Satan and the world promote—that you're not good enough so you better work harder. Get John 3:15, 16 and Matthew 11:28-30 entrenched in your spiritual outlook.

Jesus gives you a break from the horrid game of trying to become good enough and says, "Everyone who believes . . . may have eternal life" (John 3:15).

Is God Testing Me?

*I've heard many people say that God gives you prob-
lems to let you see that you need more faith. Well, I
have plenty of problems. What should I do?*

Grow in faith! I'm not trying to sound glib, but all of
us could use some faith growth.

You say you've heard many people tell you that
God gives you problems. But just because many people
have said that doesn't mean it's true.

One big source of problems is the devil. Satan, not
God, tempted Eve in the Garden of Eden (Genesis 3).
Satan is called the father of lies and a murderer from
the beginning (John 8:44). He's depicted as a roaring
lion, prowling around to devour us (1 Peter 5:8). The
Bible warns us of the great warfare between the supernatural powers of good and evil (Ephesians 6:12, 13).

But while Satan can make bad things happen
around us and to us, God can do something amazing.
He can take those bad things and turn us into someone
beautiful through them and in spite of them. (See
Romans 5:3-5.)

Another source of problems is us. Sometimes we
cause our own problems and then blame God! Adam
and Eve chose to disobey God, but then they blamed
each other and the snake instead of taking responsibility. At Mount Sinai Aaron claimed that the golden calf
just came out of the fire on its own, but the Bible says
that he took gold from the people and fashioned the
hot metal into the shape of a calf. (Compare Exodus
32:24 with verse 4 of the same chapter.)

I've heard of people who got involved in premarital

sex and then asked why God gave them a sexually transmitted disease or an unwanted pregnancy. It seems as though they chose to be sexually active, which puts them at risk for consequences.

Some people argue that God never brings bad times to people because He is the God of good. They refer to James 1:13-16, indicating that God doesn't tempt people; instead, people choose to fall into temptation as they dwell on the enticements that eventually destroy them.

Many would disagree with me, but I believe that while most of our problems are caused by the devil and ourselves, occasionally God tests us to make us more like Him. (See Exodus 14:1-4, 31 and John 11:6, 15, 42, 45 for a few examples.)

But here's what Paul said about the trials of God's people: "These things happened to them as examples and were written down as warnings for us. . . . No temptation has seized you except what is common to man. And God is faithful; he will not let you be tempted beyond what you can bear. But when you are tempted, he will also provide a way out so that you can stand up under it" (1 Corinthians 10:11-13).

I HAVE EVIL THOUGHTS

How can I eliminate evil thoughts from my mind? All kinds of negative stuff keeps bothering me.

The battle for the mind is very real! In 2 Corinthians 10:5 Paul advised, "Take captive every thought to make it obedient to Christ."

First, think about your environment and the things that precede the evil thoughts. Do the thoughts bombard you when you're inactive? If so, stay active, even if it means light activity. If you have evil thoughts when you're watching movies, then quit!

But usually there's something deeper going on that requires more than a slight behavior change. Because we're born with a sinful nature, we can come up with evil thoughts on our own!

James 1:14, 15 in *The Message* gives us a pretty graphic description of evil: "The temptation to give in to evil comes from us and only us. We have no one to blame but the leering, seducing flare-up of our own lust. Lust gets pregnant, and has a baby: sin! Sin grows up to adulthood, and becomes a real killer." So dealing with evil thoughts is a part of the Christian life.

In Luke 11:24-26 Jesus talks about a person who had a demon cast out of him (that could have included evil thoughts). Later the demon returned and found the person free and clean, but empty. So the demon gathered additional demons and returned to the man, making him worse than before—not because he'd been cleansed, but because he was still empty.

So here's another more important solution: along with avoiding situations that fuel evil thoughts, work on filling your mind with positive, godly thoughts. Let them zip through your brain and form a new groove that replaces evil thoughts.

Make sure you develop a regular habit of personal devotions. Underline portions of your Bible that you can find quickly when evil thoughts torment you. Memorize scripture.

Then when evil thoughts come to mind, pray and ask God to replace them with thoughts of His goodness. Immediately begin to praise Him for answering your prayer rather than wonder if He did. Start singing, even if you have to put on a tape or CD with religious lyrics to get you going.

Here's some encouragement from Peter. "Your life

is a journey you must travel with a deep consciousness of God. It cost God plenty to get you out of that dead-end, empty-headed life you grew up in. He paid with Christ's sacred blood." "Don't lazily slip back into those old grooves of evil, doing just what you feel like doing. You didn't know any better then; you do now. As obedient children, let yourselves be pulled into a way of life shaped by God's life, a life energetic and blazing with holiness. God said, 'I am holy; you be holy'" (1 Peter 1:18, 19, 13-16, Message).

HOW DO I SET STANDARDS?

How do you put together your own set of personal standards when the ones your parents have are different from those of your school and church?

For most people, their family provided the first set of standards for them. For example, if you grew up in a family that ate vegetarian-style, that became the standard for you. If all contemporary music was considered secular, you probably don't approve of "Christian rock." If your parents thought the King James Version of the Bible was the most accurate, you may feel suspicious of *The Message, The Clear Word,* or even the New International Version.

During the teen years most people go through a time of questioning. As teens come of age and become responsible for their own lives, they want to make sure their standards are truly their own and not just hand-me-downs from their parents. Some teens experiment with other standards, occasionally even trying the opposite of what they practiced before.

Before you choose for yourself, you want a good quantity of quality information. It can be unsettling to discover that not all adults agree on standards.

Because schools and churches are composed of many individuals and a variety of families, you should expect things at your school and church to be a little different from things at your home. Some parents set more restrictive standards for their children than the administrators of an Adventist school. Other parents seem more lenient by comparison.

Where can you go for consistency and right answers? Where is your security? Hebrews 13:8 talks about Jesus being the same "yesterday and today and forever." That's the only foundation for security.

But our understanding of Jesus changes with time, maturity, and additional information. Certainly your perception of Jesus is different now from what it was when you were a preschooler.

When you put together your own set of personal standards, try these steps:

1. ASK GOD FOR GUIDANCE.

2. GATHER INFORMATION FROM PEOPLE YOU TRUST. You can do this through personal contact and discussions.

3. BE OPEN TO CHANGE.

4. CHANGE YOUR STANDARDS ONLY WHEN A HIGHER AUTHORITY SUPPORTS IT. I'd recommend the Bible as the authority far beyond what others tell you or what you've always heard.

5. DON'T GET CAUGHT UP IN THE "CONSERVATIVE" AND "LIBERAL" DEBATE AND STEREOTYPES. Is it better to be conservative or liberal when it comes to:

    a. Giving offerings?
    b. Sexual intimacy?
    c. Forgiving others?
    d. Taking medication?
    e. Eating desserts?

Welcome to the process of making your standards your own! I'm praying for you (and others just like you) who truly want to live for Jesus!

IS ACADEMY FOR ME?

I want to go to a Seventh-day Adventist academy, but my parents say it's too expensive. What should I do? How can I know what God wants me to do?

Yes, attending an SDA academy is a big investment. You'd invest not only your money but your time. You'd probably have to get a job (or even an extra job) and spend your paycheck on tuition instead of clothes, CDs, a car, etc. So how much are you willing to invest?

Financial support may be available. But are you willing to accept help from others? (Some people aren't.)

Many academies offer students jobs to help them offset tuition. And you could ask the principal if financial aid is available. Don't expect the school just to hand out money, but sometimes funds are there for students committed to their education. SDA academies really do want students to attend!

Perhaps your local church could offer you financial support. Occasionally individual church members assist students with tuition costs too.

I attended an SDA academy and had an absolutely wonderful experience! And I know many people who say the same thing. It was in academy that Jesus became real for me. Of course, some people have negative experiences in SDA academies—let's not deny that.

But SDA academies do seek to provide an environment in which your relationship with God can flourish, and you can develop good character traits while getting an education. But what you'd gain from an SDA education would be up to you.

Frequently students who don't attend academy are forced to take a stand regarding their relationship with Christ. At a public school either you're clearly into Christ or you're not. Have you thought about how you'd handle Friday night dances, football games, Sabbath car wash fund-raisers, etc.?

Most high school-age students want to be in an environment in which they can participate in all the school events. At SDA academies students can do that without giving up or compromising their Adventist beliefs.

You also asked how to know what God wants you to do. While God doesn't usually send us notices in the mail, here's a quick four-step process I'd recommend:

1. PRAY. Hand over your life to God.

2. DO WHAT YOU CAN TO MAKE THINGS HAPPEN. Work, save money, and ask the principal or pastor for tuition assistance.

3. WATCH GOD'S MOVES. Are "doors" opening? (For example, has your church offered to cover $100 a month of your tuition bill?)

4. MAKE A DECISION. Act on what has developed, and do what you believe God wants you to.

SERVING AT HOME

Why are young people and their leaders more willing to raise money to go on mission trips than to do anything in their own church or community?

Your question makes me want to jump up and shout, "Preach it!"

I'm all for mission trips, but it's amazing that we'll

raise all kinds of money to help very needy people in another part of the earth, but we so often fail to do anything about the real and obvious needs in our own backyard.

The same kind of thing happens when people do community service activities but neglect their own family. It's like the plumber who never gets around to fixing his own pipes at home, or the pastor who tries to care for the spiritual needs of his congregation at the expense of his own spirituality.

It's inexcusable! But I think one reason we do it is that going to another country seems more exotic than helping people in our own neighborhood.

I must admit that when I go on mission trips, sometimes my good behavior comes from bad motives—"Others will think I'm terrific because I'm helping" or "I hope somebody notices how much I'm suffering just to help these people!" Remember, Isaiah wrote, "All our righteous acts are like filthy rags" (Isaiah 64:6).

But consider this: some people (certainly not all) never experience the joy of service until they're lured by the unique challenge of a mission trip. And once they've tasted of this cup, they begin looking for additional ways to maintain and even develop an unselfish lifestyle.

It's also true that some people spend loads of money on mission trips and still remain as selfish as ever, somehow failing to see that Jesus can be experienced by reaching out to "the least of these" anywhere.

When Jesus came to earth, He came without a promotional package or marketing savvy. The way Jesus treated people—what He said and how He said it—drew people to Him.

Read the story of the sheep and the goats (Matthew 25:31-46) and brainstorm some possible places around you that need Jesus. Then go do something about it!

(But don't forget to help sponsor teens going on

mission trips. For some it seems to be the only way to jump-start a life of service.)

PREPARING FOR THE LAST DAYS

How can teenagers (and people in general)
prepare for the "last days"?

G reat question! And depending upon whom you ask, you're apt to get a variety of answers, such as:

• Become perfect (completely without sin).

• Get a good hideout in the mountains and start stashing away food (you're out of luck if you live in a flat state such as Kansas!).

• Study prophecy more closely so you'll have a better idea when the end really is coming.

• Drop out of school and hit the road, telling everyone you meet that Jesus is coming soon.

• Preach a "John the Baptist message" that turns the hearts of the parents to their children and the hearts of the children to their parents.

• Be more serious about your relationship with God, because there just isn't any more time to be messing around.

• Keep up-to-date on news headlines and compare them with Bible prophecies.

• Shake the sinners out of your church so Jesus can come to get the righteous.

• Pray more and wait for God to tell you what to do.

• Do nothing.

Because you sent your question to me, though, I'll tell you what I believe people should do to prepare for the "last days."

In Matthew 24 Jesus talked about some warning

135

signs for when the fall of Jerusalem would take place and also when the end of the world would come. We use this chapter to identify some of the signs of Christ's second coming.

As far as I'm concerned, the only sign left to be fulfilled is the one described in Matthew 24:14: "And this gospel of the kingdom will be preached in the whole world as a testimony to all nations, and then the end will come."

I don't think we've finished sharing the good news about Jesus throughout the entire world. And God could handle that instantly if He wanted to.

In discussions about the last days, though, people often overlook the connection between Matthew 24 (signs of Christ's coming) and Matthew 25 (how to be ready for Christ's coming).

Matthew 25 contains three well-known stories that give us clues for preparing for Christ's return. I suggest that you read this chapter as well as some great comments on it in the books *Christ's Object Lessons* (pp. 405-421 and 325-365) and *The Desire of Ages* (pp. 637-641).

The first story is about 10 bridesmaids—five foolish and five wise. The difference is that half of them have only enough oil for a little while in contrast to those who have oil to last much longer. The oil represents the Holy Spirit in a person's life.

Those who are content with just a little bit of the Holy Spirit evidently won't last very long. The way to prepare is to not only invite the Holy Spirit into your life, but to consistently ask and be open to the Holy Spirit transforming your life so you become more and more like Jesus. Because our sinful nature drags us toward selfishness, we're in need of the constant impact of the Holy Spirit to keep changing us.

Please note that both sets of bridesmaids had oil and both sets fell asleep. The difference was whether or not they were superficial or serious about their Christianity.

The second story in Matthew 25 tells about three servants who received various amounts of talents. Those who use what they are given are rewarded. The one who doesn't use what he's been given gets left out.

The talent(s) includes money, but also much more, such as the spiritual gifts God gives and other talents given to each person. Special mention is made in *Christ's Object Lessons* about the talents of thinking, speaking, influence, time, health, strength, and kindness.

From a human perspective, the more talents a person has, the better that person is. But from God's view, the number of talents doesn't matter. What counts to God is that people develop the talents He has given them.

What can people do to prepare for the last days? Develop the talents God has already given them. By the way, there's no indication that people should be old to develop their talents. In fact, if anything, it's especially true for young people to develop what God has given them now. Regardless of whether or not others think you're capable, ask God to work in you to develop the talents He has given you right where you are now!

The third story is the familiar one about the sheep and goats. The summary of this story is that on judgment day, God will be able to separate the sheep (His people) and goats (those who aren't His people) based on what they've done to serve others. What seems to surprise everyone is that they didn't actually know the people they were helping were Jesus.

Don't be confused that helping others saves you. It's just one of the obvious ways to tell that Jesus has already saved you—you end up living for others instead of just living for yourself. Pretty obvious, huh? Want to see Jesus? Then check out those who need help. This can include the homeless, rejects, fanatics, nobodies, those who are abused, neglected, sick, terminally ill, rich, depressed, religious, even those who seem popular—whoever needs help.

How can people prepare for the last days? Keep having the Holy Spirit transform them to become more and more like Jesus, develop the talents God has given them right where they are, and help everyone they can however they can.

See you in heaven, and I'll look for you acting heavenly right now, because heaven will be living out of your heart and life!

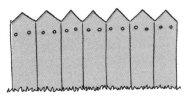

Conclusion

I'VE GOT A FEW QUESTIONS FOR YOU.

1. What's going on with you and Jesus right now? Please explain.

2. If things continue the way they're going, where will you be in your relationship with Jesus three months from now?

3. Who can you talk to about spiritual things?

4. Is your religion mainly your parents' religion or has it become your own choice? What makes it that way? How do you know?

5. What do you do for a devotional life?

6. What are you doing in service for others (because if you aren't giving to others, you'll die spiritually)?

7. What do you want to do before Jesus returns?

8. Who are your heroes? Who are your mentors?

9. What has God given you to reach others with the good news about Jesus?

10. Do you go to church to get something or to give something?

11. What do you do with the gift (called "the Sabbath") that God has given you?

12. Who are the people that look up to you? How aware have you been that people do look up to you?

13. What keeps you going in your Christian walk?

14. Do you have a place where you can ask questions?

15. Do you know where to find answers?

16. Do you have a foundation of trust in God to see you through the times when you don't see answers to some of your questions?

SCRIPTURE INDEX

143